DEREK JONES' COUNTRY BOOK

DEREK JONES' COUNTRY BOOK

With Illustrations by
NORMAN HICKIN

DAVID & CHARLES
NEWTON ABBOT LONDON NORTH POMFRET (VT)

ISBN 0 7153 6963 6
Library of Congress Catalog Card Number 74–33155

Photoset and printed in Great Britain by
REDWOOD BURN LTD Trowbridge & Esher
for David & Charles (Holdings) Limited
South Devon House Newton Abbot Devon

Published in the United States of America
by David & Charles Inc
North Pomfret Vermont 05053 USA

To my wife and willing secretary
ANGELA

Contents

Illustrations

Introduction

If there's one sure way to get to know something of the country-side, it is to mix with real countrymen, hanging on their every word, watching their every move, and responding instantly to that gentle touch on the shoulder which means 'Freeze!'

I learnt my first, crucial lessons as an eager youngster dogging the footsteps of my father and grandfather, who were both game-keepers, across Welsh hills, Herefordshire woodlands and Somer-set fields. By the time that I was five, I was being paid for this doggedness; I would line up with the beaters for a day's pay, earning half a crown for a little beating, and a lot of cartridge-case collecting. A few years later, I 'loaded' for the syndicate-boss's son —another cushy job, since he only had one gun. Nevertheless, carrying his cartridge bag brought in half a crown as well.

The end of the shooting season heralded the inevitable round of vermin-trapping. This was another business which taught me a lot; from how to set rabbit snares and bait traps, to how to tell whether a vixen's earth was occupied. There was, of course friendly rivalry among us youngsters; to be the first to spot a songbird's nest; and, in those days, to have the best collection of birds' eggs. Indeed, at that age, my love of the countryside was inspired as much by youthful exhilaration, by a sense of challenges to be overcome, as by a desire simply to look and learn.

Guns are a traditional accoutrement for men living in the country, and I vividly remember my first encounter with a gun, a .410, which I managed to aim more or less accurately at a house sparrow's nest. My last outing with a gun is an equally clear memory—of a day spent waiting for a sight of a pheasant, and of a single, brief opportunity for a shot. Since that day, however, I have used the patience and alertness that I had learned, to gain a rather different kind of satisfaction from the countryside.

My outlook and intentions may have changed, the shotgun and the snares may have been replaced by the binoculars and the tape-recorder, but the important thing—the countryside—is the same. Much of my work now is done with the BBC Natural History Unit for the radio programmes 'The Living World' and 'Wildlife'. In that respect, I feel rather like the poacher who became a keeper, but what I learned about the countryside in earlier days has certainly stood me in good stead now that part of my living depends on it.

This book, like the course of my life, is a mixture of old tricks put to new uses, or rather old experiences given new applications.

The idea for the book was inspired originally by the series of three-minute talks broadcast on BBC Radio Bristol. One or two of these same topics, unharassed by time, that arch-enemy of man and broadcaster, appear in the following chapters. Indeed, without the stimulus of having to find a different subject each week for Radio Bristol, I should never have been moved to tackle a book.

Broadcasting on natural history and the countryside provided me not only with stimulation but with education. Working with real experts, the botanists, zoologists and entomologists in 'The Living World' and 'Wildlife', has greatly extended my learning and knowledge. To all of them I extend my thanks. And to some my apologies for putting awkward questions when they least expected them. They may not, however, read these words, for this is strictly a book for the non-ologist, written by a non-ologist. It simply expresses the thoughts of a countryman, nonetheless a countryman who tries to go around with his eyes not only open but seeing and, in seeing, understanding.

Secrecy or Selfishness

A dilemma that all of us are faced with when we make a new and exciting discovery, is whether to share the secret or keep it to ourselves; should we savour what it has to offer or tell the world, let it become common property, and so risk destroying our private paradise.

I know a certain spot and there was a time when wild horses wouldn't have drawn me to tell exactly where it is. It's one of those areas of the countryside that are fast disappearing in the face of the need to make every acre show a profit on the balance sheet. In fact, it is not much more than a couple of acres of absolutely useless land tucked in a fold in the hills, wet, boggy in places, and becoming overgrown with alder trees. Occasionally cattle break into it to find shelter from the summer sun, but precious little in the way of grazing.

Reaching it calls for wellington boots, a stout stick and more than a little resolution to fight your way through the thick undergrowth of a lane long since fallen into disuse. In places the lane has given way to a stream, and it's the water from this stream that makes the secret spot so marshy.

Difficult though the journey is, once a year, come high summer, it's an expedition that has to be made for the sights and the scents. This bog, in most years, is covered with patches of scented wild orchids, their purples contrasting with the creamy white of clumps of marsh helleborine, another member of the orchid family. That very strange two leafed orchid, the twayblade, and that other lover of damp places, the bogbean are also to be found there.

So there it is, this secret place known to a handful of, perhaps, selfish people who go there once a year to revel in the colours and the scents. Others may well know it, but have never been there when it blossoms, for a few short weeks, into a splendid botanical paradise. This is the dilemma. Is paradise personal and secret, or should it be shared?

I know the problem only too well. Tell, and the place will be invaded and destroyed. Yet, at the same time, it is destroying itself as, slowly but surely, the alder trees spread further through the bog, making too much shade for some of the flowers. They are changing it from a damp old bit of what was once pasture land, into a sour place where, eventually, nothing will grow except the alders. It's the sort of place that knowledgeable botanists should study before it's too late. That bog needs to be managed today if it is to be of any value at all, for once let it be drained and the orchids will no longer bloom every summer.

The question of secrecy is not confined to areas of interest to the botanists, it applies equally to ornithology. There was a time, many years ago, when my father found a raven's nest high in the hills of Radnorshire. Unfortunately, by the time that he made the discovery, the secret was already known—others had arrived in those far hills looking for just such a nest.

It takes no great skill to track down the nest site of such grand birds. They give themselves away by their splendid flight and an-nounce their territory with that beautiful guttural call that is as dis-

tinctive as a foghorn to a mariner. Once heard, once seen, the raven's nest can soon be found. That is not usually the end of the problem, since ravens nest in the most inaccessible places.

In the case of my father's bird it was not so, the tree could be climbed. Having found the nest as well, the egg-collector kept it under observation until a full clutch had been laid. It didn't take a great detective to realise that at the first opportunity they would be up the tree and away with the eggs.

Now not even the keenest conservationist can keep one nest under observation around the clock, and so, rather than allow those eggs to be taken and sold, father took the eggs himself and they found a place in our collection. Had the nest not been found by the collectors those eggs would have remained undisturbed. It was a difficult decision, but on reflection, the right one.

Ravens are not the only birds to give themselves away. Herons are equally obvious and on one occasion betrayed themselves to me. For some days I had seen herons returning from the flats and marshes, and I assumed they were making their way back to a heronry well known in the locality. However, one or two evenings later, I had a doubt in my mind, because they seemed to be flying in quite the wrong direction. I thought no more about it for several days until an evening stroll with no particular object in mind took me into a woodland, tall, and dark with larch trees.

There in this plantation, I suddenly heard the clacking sound that could only be young herons and, sure enough, right above my head, high in the larch, I saw the great stick platform that is the herons' nest. It is on occasions like this that stealth is important, and I left the wood as quickly and as quietly as I could. Despite this, several herons were disturbed and took flight for a few minutes, slowly circling back to their nests.

My coming and going had not gone unnoticed. The good people who live by the plantation hailed me and soon told me more about their heronry. It started only four years ago with one pair, and today there are some five nests high in the trees. The birds give these people immense pleasure and they invited me to come and watch their growing colony. There was, however, one proviso in that invitation. 'Don't spread it around', they said, 'we don't want the place swarming with bird watchers'.

Their secret is still secure with me, but herons are herons as ravens are ravens, and it can't stay secret for long. These birds announce their coming and their going, and local ornithologists probably know about the heronry anyway, but being responsible people, are not shouting the news from the rooftops either.

Read the Signs

There was a time, not so very long ago, when golf was a passion in my life, and took me out onto courses in all winds and weathers. Even now, as the shafts of the irons and woods go rusty in the garage, many of the more subtle rules of the game stay with me, like the one about 'obtaining relief if your ball comes to rest in a rabbit scrape'. Golf courses, being what they are, have, in many cases, healthy populations of rabbits. Rabbits, being what they are, wander out on the fairways to feed on the lush, green grass, scratching out shallow indentations in the turf, and leaving their droppings by those scrapes. There are many sharp-practising golfers, who, finding their ball on a slightly bare patch of ground, claim that it is resting in a rabbit scrape, when the hole actually isn't even deep enough to have been made by the snout of a shrew or the footprint of a mole!

The marks left by rabbits are among the more obvious signs left by animals in the countryside, but I have known these scrapes to be confused with those of badgers. After all, they do serve the same purpose, but the badger latrine is a deeper scar in the soil and Brock, being such a clean animal, more often than not, covers his excreta afterwards. But, find a haphazard collection of these small indentations in a woodland, or the edge of a field, and you won't have to look very far for the badger set. A well defined path, a few inches wide, will lead you straight to one of the several entrances.

Badgers leave other very distinctive evidence around their doorsteps, particularly when they change their bedding. The entrance to the set is often several inches deep in a mixture of soil and dead grass or bracken. The whole lot is bundled out into a small hillock, and the signs of the new material having been taken into the hole are just as clear. The path followed by the animal from a clump of bracken, or from the edge of a field, with its load of bedding, looks rather like the passage of an old hay cart along a narrow lane. There, strands of the harvest are left clinging to the hedgerows, so with the foraging of the badger, debris from the haycart in miniature litters its path.

There is one other sign that calls for a bit of detective work before you can be certain of the culprit. It's often to be found under beech trees or in hazel coppices; a neat round hole, which looks for all the world as if a pint-sized potter had been smoothing round the soil as he would a lump of clay on his wheel. This hole, quite circular and barely a couple of inches across, is the work of that arch tree-rodent, the grey squirrel, trying to find a beech or hazel nut. Some birds too, leave distinctive visiting cards. The disturbance of leaves under beech or oak trees usually means a pigeon has been scratching around for a meal, while leaves moved from the surface of the soil into a roughly circular dish, the size of a soup plate, indicate that a blackbird has been searching for worms or insects.

Reading the signs of the countryside really is detective work, and in some cases the theories which lie behind criminal investigation apply, because once there is a 'record', and a known modus operandi, you have something to work on, and once a sign is recognised for what it is, there is no need to look any further.

Take those super countryside criminals, foxes. The cubs are extraordinarily playful creatures, and, once the vixen has moved them from the small hole where the litter was born to a more substantial earth, they are as full of vitality as the pups of our own domestic dogs. One of their principal games is a sort of 'tag', usually played around an ant hill or a large clump of grass. In their chasing each other, they leave the surrounding vegetation flattened in a well-defined track, as clear as the meandering course of motor-cycle scramble competitors. Day after day the cubs play, round and round the same spot, and once you've seen such a playground, you need no second opinion. Fox cubs were the culprits.

There's another sight not very often seen, even by the keenest investigator of the countryside, but one that's more common than any other evidence left by an otter. Most people wouldn't give a second glance, to that gentle, smooth, sandy slope from the river bank down to the water's edge. But when you remember that otters 'toboggan' from river bank to the water just below, the signs tell all. These telltale signs take a lot of finding, and like so many secrets of the countryside, are seldom given up to the man who goes out looking for them deliberately. It is the chance discovery that is the reward for real observation.

Equally unobtrusive too, is the work of another very shy animal. You might find the evidence in a sheltered spot; among carpets of pine needles in a plantation; in the middle of a clump of dead bracken; under a rhododendron bush; even in the dead grass in the corner of a quiet field, but always in a quiet sheltered spot. The ground may be slightly, very slightly flattened, covering an area of about two and a half feet by eighteen inches. Just look at it and you'll see that the ground is not only flattened, but that there is the faintest suggestion of a hollow, as if something fairly heavy had been lying there, like the shape left by a dog when it curls up in a bed of straw.

This, however, was not the work of any dog. You're looking at the spot where a roe deer has been resting. They lay up for hours in spots like this, and you might have been very close to actually seeing the deer before your coming disturbed it. If that hollow is still warm to the touch of your hand, you only missed seeing the deer by a matter of seconds.

The greatest pleasure about this sort of detection is that it is possible to make a comprehensive list of many of the inhabitants of a particular area, without ever meeting them face to face. Once you've got to know the signs that's really all you need; it's then a question of keen eyesight and an ability to interpret a series of clues that, individually, may seem insignificant, but together, add up to a complete casebook with a very clear signature on each and every page.

Owl

It all began really as a hunch, a conviction that we had moved into owl country. We found this house in a North Somerset village, a real village with a green and a pub. It was farming country with a new motorway, near enough for the convenience of long-distance travelling, far enough away for any noise to be reduced to a mild rumble.

Owl number one soon made its presence heard, right on the roof early one morning, a tawny owl which got an answering call away in the woods above the hillside opposite. That hillside is dotted with old trees, oak and ash, gnarled and twisted with age, many of them rotten and hollow. It was ideal owl territory, but it wasn't the tawny owl that interested me. I had the feeling that if a barn owl should be around, the pickings here would be ideal. There was plenty of pasture, there were mature plantations, old trees galore and the motorway embankments, and so the search began.

I looked high and low among the hollow trees. I kept my ears tuned for any sound, not just of a barn owl itself. I kept my ears also open for local talk—where local talk is best heard, in the pub across the green. Sure enough, one evening, someone, unaware even of my interest, was heard to remark that he'd seen a white owl on the by-pass.

At last one night, the evidence came home to roost. Just as it had with the tawny owl, the roof of the house became a temporary and brief song post, or rather screech post. We heard the unmistakable and terrifying screech of a barn owl. After this episode, I redoubled my efforts, going around all those old trees on the hillside again and again. But nothing, not a feather, not a dropping, not a pellet was to be seen.

The progress, or rather lack of progress, of my search provided yet another illustration of the naturalist's adage, that you never find what you're looking for, until you stop trying. The most exciting discoveries always come when you least expect them. I was eventually successful at a place that I had dismissed as being too noisy; it seemed far too near the motorway and was frequented by that noisy bird, the jackdaw. On the site in question stood an old yew tree, 900 years old according to the parish records, now moribund and little more than a skeleton.

When I first noticed an ebony-black dropping about the size of a thumb at the base of the tree, I thought that a dog had passed that way. Then I saw a bone protruding from the capsule and, close by it, two similar capsules. These were, of course, three barn owl casts or pellets.

From that day on, through the winter, I paid regular visits to the old yew tree. I went every day for a while, trying to do it as inconspicuously as possible, by turns as furtively as a poacher, or as nonchalantly as a keeper looking at his tunnel traps when he thinks he's being watched. I gave this up for two reasons.

First of all, I felt like the driver of a security van trying to take a different route every day; secondly, the barn owl didn't often reward me. I would see nothing for day after day, then, maybe on the fourth day, three or four pellets at the base of the tree would repay my visit.

Having tracked down my barn owl and collected the circumstantial evidence, I decided then to try and find out what it was eating. Taking the barn owl pellets apart is not the filthy job it might seem. All that the owl has done, is to remove all the flesh from its prey by the digestive juices in its stomach, and then to regurgitate the remains as a small black parcel with all the tiny bones cleanly wrapped in a soft container of fur.

The best place for the job is the kitchen sink, though tact must be exercised to placate the family. You will need a pair of tweezers and a large needle. I've found that the easiest way to take the pellets apart is to put each one in a plastic tray, the sort used for potted plants. Soak each pellet in warm water, leave it for a few minutes, then drain off the water, and, with the tweezers and needle, tease the bones and fur apart. Separate, piece by piece, all the tiny bones, some of which will be infinitesimally small. Place the bones in another dish of clean water, drain that away, and leave them by the kitchen boiler to dry.

This is a time-consuming but rewarding job because there, in each pellet, is the evidence of what the barn owl has been eating. Each pellet tells a different story, and the skulls and bones of the small mammals provide a detailed catalogue of the bird's diet. Meticulous as I was in my probings, I probably missed a bone or two, even in the bonanza pellet that yielded 401 bones, including eight skulls. This pellet was particularly interesting in that one end of it was not ebony-black, but bright pink—flesh from the nose of a vole. It seems that, on this occasion, the owl had eaten more than its fill, and was unable to fully digest the last part of its meal.

The results of this head-count are most interesting. Of thirty pellets sampled during ten weeks from the end of November, the average contents work out at 3.1 small mammals per pellet. Voles make up the principal source of food—almost 90 per cent. The remains of common and pigmy shrews were also found and, from the pellets sampled in January, the remains of two rats.

There was, significantly, not a sign of the bones of any small birds. It's generally reckoned that a barn owl produces two pellets per day, and I thought, for a while, that my owl might have another daytime roost, since I was collecting only about four or five pellets per week. I have now discovered that this particular yew tree was in fact used by the owl as its nest site last year. Therefore, many of its pellets are being deposited around the nest area itself, inside the tree. What I pick up at the base is obviously the overflow. So the amateur research will continue through the year. Having once tracked this barn owl down, I feel that I know him fairly well. The pattern has been that of a detective story, but a story in which the detective collects clues about a subject that he has never seen. Still I know that the bird is there, and that is all that matters.

'Keep Out'

The gulf of distrust between town and country seems to increase with every passing year, and by the middle of each summer becomes a veritable Cheddar Gorge. Come the holiday season, when more and more people get into their cars to explore the countryside, it's brought home forcibly to the farmer that, although his home is his castle, in the eyes of some people, his gardens are not. No matter what efforts he makes to maintain his privacy, to keep his property enclosed, to keep his sheep and cattle in his fields—and they are after all his gardens—there are always thoughtless wanderers who abuse that privacy.

The average farmer is a tolerant, well disposed and amiable chap, and he will approach the miscreants politely, but, just now and again, even his patience runs out. He tries attack, verbal attack, and tells the trespassers that if they insist on trampling over his corn, he sees no reason why he shouldn't come along and walk his cattle through their gardens. Perhaps the point gets home, for there is no difference in principle. Couldn't you just hear the threats of court action and compensation, if the roses were to be mangled by cows? But then your semi-detached surburban is not the same as the farm, it has a notice: 21 Camellia Drive; Chez Nous; La Casita; Adobe Hacienda; or inevitably Issners. There's a name to the place, and that means, in so many words, keep out, this is ours.

Some countrymen do the same thing, but the notice actually spells 'Keep Out'. It's a desperates move forced by years of battle confrontation. It used to be, 'Please Keep Out'. Now it is 'Shut The Gate'; the polite preface has become another casualty of the conflict. The most effective deterrent is a few strands of rusty barbed wire woven through the cross-bars of the gate, with the gate itself padlocked against invaders.

I get the feeling that perhaps we've become immune to signs. It can't all be put down to illiteracy. Take the case of the Ministry of Transport sign; high, wide and far from handsome, it stands blue and white, covered with words and diagrams, on the outskirts of our village. For some reason many motorists read it wrongly and belt into the village, fondly thinking they are heading towards that blissful holiday highroad, the motorway. They just haven't taken in the information given by the benevolent ministry, and, instead of finding themselves in seventy-on-the-clock territory, they screech to a tyre-destroying halt in a cul-de-sac.

There was a time when we used to respect 'Please Keep Off The Grass'. That was a tiny notice compared with the twelve foot square road-sign yet it had more impact. This wasn't only because there might have been an aggressive park keeper hovering in wait behind a rhododendron bush either, so perhaps it's the psychology of signs that bears looking at more closely. There was an air of authority about, 'Trespassers Will Be Prosecuted', but these days its impact seems to have waned, perhaps because the trespasser realises that few land-owners would bother with the expense of actually bringing a prosecution.

One of the most effective country signs used to be, 'Beware of the Bull.' No 'please' about it, the choice was entirely up to the walker, and, if the sign was backed by a fearsome looking beast in the middle of the field, it certainly worked. The sad fact that the animal's only pretentions to being a bull had disappeared long ago didn't matter. 'Bull' it said, bull it looked like, and we kept out. Today though, the knowledgeable and determined countryside explorer briefly considers the situation, and reflects that very few farmers keep bulls these days, relying instead for procreation of their herds on the Artificial Insemination Service. It can't be a bull he reasons, so into the field he goes. In a few instances of course, he realises the error of his ways, when the thundering, bellowing beast proclaims in no uncertain terms that it is indeed a bull.

There was a most interesting sign some years ago that used to work for the farmer when it came to the casual passer-by, but had not the slightest effect on the locals. The sign indicated that one particular field contained cultivated mushrooms. Well, it saved some of the plentiful supply of the wild crop for the farmer, but everyone in the area knew that he hadn't really planned to have mushrooms on those particular acres, he was just trying to keep some of his good fortune to himself.

Still, the sign worked up to a point, and there's another we know only too well in the Mendip Hills in Somerset. It is quite simple and very much to the point: 'Danger, Adders.' Now some people might interpret that as meaning that predatory mathematicians abound in the area. Others, knowing full well that, there have indeed been cases of snake-bite on those hills, take it at its face value. Yet it is probably true that some farmers put up the notice merely as a deterrent, and it's certainly effective.

So perhaps these days we have so many notices and signs everywhere we go, that we don't take in the messages they are designed to convey. The notice that needs a second look seems the most effective; the one you think reads, 'Police Notice, No Parking,' until you take a second glance, and realise it is really, 'Polite Notice, No Parking.' Sadly, this kind is becoming so common now that their effect is weakened. The most graphic message I've ever seen was on the Continent, directed at members of the American forces. A mangled wreck of a car lay by the side of the road, left where it had crashed with inevitable loss of life. The message above it read simply 'Death Is So Permanent.'

Butterfly Hill

One of the unfortunate things about the march of progress is that its route often takes it across open country and farmland. What were once flourishing market gardens cease to provide food as developers move in and, providing the planners have given their gracious consent, tracts of agricultural land give up their greenery to the grey concrete and drab blocks of stone of another housing estate. We all need a roof over our heads and a place to work, so the land must be found somewhere. If a farmer or market gardener, in his later years, can see a better income from capital than from slogging at the soil, then why shouldn't he sell up? The land to satisfy our needs must come from somewhere, and, short of giant reclamation schemes, the nibbling away at what we have got will continue.

There are, thankfully, some stretches of 'our green and pleasant land' that, even in the wildest imagination, will never be more that what they are today. In building terms these areas are impossible;

31

from an agricultural viewpoint, barely marginal. On the surface, these places are hardly worth a second glance, but, for all that, they can be important wildlife reservoirs.

Just such a place is a hillock I know, a solid lump of limestone that rises steeply above the surrounding countryside. It's dotted with old oaks and elms, some of them rotten with age and weather. Brambles, blackthorn, thistles and king-size nettles bar the way; bushes of hawthorn push root systems deep down into the cracks in the rock and there's enough grass of a sort to support a small herd of store cattle, provided their rations are eked out with a supply of

hay. It's wild, unkempt, and full of what any self-respecting farmer would call weeds. But when we remember that weeds are really only wild plants growing where we don't want them, this hillock takes on a new importance.

Every time I wander over it to the summit, following the narrow tracks made through the brambles and nettles by the cattle, I rejoice because it's a paradise for insect life. Being the sort of ground it is, I can't see it ever being sprayed with insecticides or herbicides, and so it stands a very good chance of remaining unspoilt. The foraging cattle do all the cropping that's necessary. Some of it doesn't need any control at all, simply because of the very geology of the place; the rocky outcrops barely permit any growth but that of wild thyme, and beautiful carpets of it creep over the limestone in patchwork quilting of purple and green. And now and again may be seen the tall, slender spikes of that plant of waste ground, the mullein, with its soft velvet-grey foliage and yellow flowers. There too, ragwort finds space and a place in the order of things on the hill.

So the insects thrive and, particularly, the butterflies. The first to appear, the over-wintering species apart, are clouds of orange tips —the first hatch of early summer. As the days get longer and warmer, and then decline, so the hill takes on the butterfly pattern that used to be so common, but now, alas, is the exception rather than the rule. I've walked this place, and given up counting numbers, concentrating only on species; large whites, small whites, meadow browns, large tortoiseshells, red admirals, the splendid peacock, and that ragged looking comma are all to be seen. The painted lady appears too, and some of those smaller butterflies that are as difficult to tell apart as those 'small brown jobs' of the ornithologists' world, the warblers.

That common ragwort which most farmers hate, later in the year also takes on a ragged look, as the caterpillar that looks like a colourful concertina, with it's black and orange stripes, eats its way through the foliage. This is the caterpillar of the cinnabar moth, the lovely red and black insect which flies by day or night. In this ragwort lies the clue to the success and importance of my hillock, because there are so many so-called weeds that are vitally important to butterflies and moths—some as feed plants, others as plants where the insects lay their eggs. Many of these insects are specific in their plant needs, and if the plants are absent, killed off by herbicides, then the insects too are doomed.

Many of us are getting the message about planting butterfly

magnets in our gardens, like buddleias and michaelmas daisies, and leaving the odd clump of nettles too, but my hill is an instance of natural magnetism, a bit of the country left to its own devices and gone wild.

It's a wilderness, yet, at the same time, a stage on which is played out the summer's gay pageant; as the butterflies dance in the spotlight of the sun to the accompaniment of the musicians of this open-air production, the grasshoppers. May this entertainment never end its run. If it does, we, the patrons, shall be to blame.

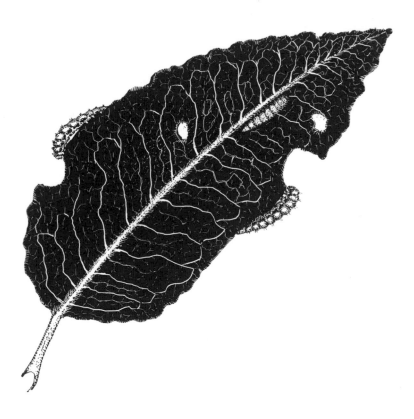

You Need Your Ormer 'Ook

There's something of the beachcomber in all of us. We all pick up shells and stones from favourite holiday beaches, stuff them away in drawers until the annual spring-clean consigns them to the rubbish bin. It takes all sorts: bits of granite and sandstone, shells of whelk and limpet and periwinkle, rocks as smooth and polished as precious stones, a bit of old brick sculpted by sand and tide into a miniature Henry Moore.

I've got quite a collection of them, picked up on my travels through the country, and I can look at them today and remember when and where I found them. Perhaps I should have explained that all these trinkets also used to fill odd spaces in drawers and cupboards, until there came a move that can only be described as desperate. I was duly presented with a couple of tall glass jars with cork stoppers. They now contain shells and stones, and most elegant ornaments they make, with the added advantage of leaving drawers and cupboards available for their real purpose.

To bring out all the natural colours of the collection, the best effect is obtained if the jars are filled with clean water, but a word of warning. From time to time nature takes over and a green alga grows on the stones and shells. Then there's nothing for it but to empty the whole lot into the sink, and thoroughly clean them. If a dash of mild kitchen bleach is added to the water, this keeps the alga at bay.

Most of my beachcombing has been done on remote beaches, and at the time of the year when the holiday makers have gone home, with their memories of golden sands and blistering sunshine to see them through the winter. It's only then, when the oystercatchers whistle their way above the low tide line, and the turnstones strut and flip through the washed up weed that a favourite beach shows up its real character.

It's worth going back to those spots you remember as being full of colourful awnings and sunshades and roadside cafes where you could quench a summer thirst. Now the shutters are up and sandbags line the streets. They guard every doorway along the Esplanade in St. Helier, Jersey, for instance, as shopkeepers and businessmen and houseowners put up the barricades against the spring tides. But the tides that sometimes invade their homes give Channel Islanders a bonus to offset the inconvenience of sandbags on their doorsteps and seaweed in their gardens. For, just as the spring tides of winter flow exceptionally high, so the ebb parts of the shoreline are revealed as a new and exciting world, only exposed on a few days in the year—a vista of rock-pinnacles, never seen by the holidaymaker, rising above fields of oar-weed. As that tide recedes, so local people put on their waders and their oldest clothes, and crowd to the edge of the water. They all have their favourite traditional spots, and they busy themselves among the rocks and pools, thigh-high in the water, peering about, groping under the rocks up to their armpits. They are collecting ormers.

The ormer is a shell fish related to the limpet and the abalone. It's a Mediterranean species, and it's northern limits are the Channel Islands. There in Jersey, Guernsey, Sark, Alderney and Herm, ormer shells are used for decorative purposes, and may be seen set into walls and masonry, glistening many coloured as the sun picks out their subtle shades. This beautiful shell, with its delicately colourful mother of pearl interior, owes its name, which comes from the french *oreille de mer*, to its ear-like shape. Although they do find a market in the trinket shops and fish stalls, it's not for the shells that the Channel Islanders collect their ormers; the shell is the by-product, the real meat is the mollusc itself. So off they go ormering with a small bag and ormer hook. The hook is necessary because it's impossible to prise the ormer off the rocks without some sort of leverage, although any short iron bar will do the trick. The bag of course, is used to carry the catch.

I've talked to some of these prospectors as they've returned from their forays, but you never get much information. There's a natural reticence among them, in striking contrast to the tales of the fishermen using rod and line; only the old bag or bit of sacking bulging and dripping wet, tells the true story that enough ormers have been collected for a meal. Don't be misled by the appearance of these gourmets. Old clothes and leaky waders they may have, but the average ormerer is just as likely to deposit his bag in the boot of an XJ12 or a Bentley, as he is to throw it into the back of a rusty Renault.

I know my many friends in the islands will forgive me, but I have yet to appreciate fully this shell fish they describe in such glowing terms as a delicacy. As far as I can make out from my introduction to it, the meat is first prised from the shell and scrubbed with a very hard scrubbing brush. Then it's walloped, that is, beaten with a rolling pin in the way that some people tenderise steak, and that isn't the end of the process by any means. Indeed, it might be better to come back for the meal tomorrow because the ormers are then fried and browned in butter. The next stage is to place them in a casserole with, I believe, onions and herbs. That little preparation has to bake for hours and hours.

Such a dish was prepared for me with loving care, and it was presented with a flourish that couldn't have been bettered by a head waiter at any of the plusher hotels in Guernsey. You could see the rest of the guests, islanders, eager to sample the first of the season's ormers. Maybe it's an acquired taste, and again my apologies to my very good friends, but to me it was rather like eating slightly tough veal that had a distinctly fishy flavour. Of course the holiday season is not the ormer season, but significantly, even at those hotels that do expect a few visitors in the winter months, I have never once seen ormers on the menu.

Islanders will tell you perhaps that there aren't enough ormers to go round, and indeed it is true that, from time to time, bans have to be put on the taking of ormers because their numbers have declined. The blame for this is often put on the people who go skin diving and who, with the protection of their wet suits and aqualungs, are able to get to those very spots that are only exposed at low tides. They undoubtedly have reaped a certain harvest, but I sometimes wonder whether the traditional ormerers are not themselves to blame. The attack they make on the well known ormer areas is relentless, and no stone that might conceal an ormer is left unturned. The disturbance is tremendous, particularly as each area is not the preserve of any one man.

I was always taught that any stone moved on a shore line should be replaced, because every rock in the water is in effect, a mini ecosystem. Anything that lives in such an environment is perfectly capable of dealing with the movement produced by the sea, but take a rock from the water and let it dry in the sun for an hour, and some life-forms will perish. Once this happens, the delicate interdependant balance is upset and the system will break down. It's something for Channel Islanders, who may be without their favourite dish this year to, chew over.

Watchdog of the Countryside

The gamekeeper's gibbet is not a pretty sight. A line of rotting fly-blown corpses are left drying out in the sun, some of them so decomposed as to be hardly recognisable unless you're a keen eyed zoologist. Careful examination might reveal carrion crows, magpies, jays, stoats, weasels, hedgehogs, moles and rats. You may even come across, owls, sparrow hawks, kestrels and buzzards, but in these days a man would be a fool to leave such damning evidence lying around.

The gibbet is no purpose built device. Any old stretch of barbed wire on which the corpses can be strung will do. Nor will it be there for all to see. It's usually to be found deep in the estate, next to the keeper's cabin, a spot where only he and perhaps his employer would venture. Yet, just occasionally, a rambler wanders off the beaten track and finds himself in such a spot, confronted by the gibbet. Then the cries of anguish echo through the correspondence columns of the national press. The keeper is castigated, his employer maligned, and the public image of a man who is really a public servant drops back into the trough that has been for so long his lonely lot.

In many respects, however, this is not the fault of the keeper, it's the fault of the system and society. Until the outbreak of the war in 1939, the average keeper, a head keeper at that, was on farm labouring wages, say fifty shillings a week. Admittedly like a farm labourer, he had a cottage provided, and very often a most habitable affair it was. Yet, as befitted his life, it was a lonely, inaccessible place miles from anywhere. True, he was probably also provided with one suit a year, and none of your fifty shilling tailors—the finest Harris tweed, made to measure.

The man got a suit to fit his station, because the good keeper was respected in the countryside. He was the next in line after the village policeman, and like the policeman he was never off duty. His was a year-round profession, with perhaps a visit to Cruft's Dog Show at the end of the shooting season, followed, perhaps, by a week's holiday that could only be taken at the most inhospitable time of the year, when the chill winds and snows of February blew his remaining pheasants back to shelter in the cover of his woodlands. Once that holiday was over, it was on with the annual spring attack on the vermin, indeed on with the battle against anything likely to prey on pheasants or partridges at any stage during their precarious lives.

The reasons for this spring campaign were two-fold. In the first place any keeper who, having been provided with three thousand pheasant eggs in the spring, could only show a few hundred high-flying birds in the shooting season, would be out of a job. He was either a poacher who had never reformed, or else a bad keeper, and his chances of getting another position with those references would have been nil. Secondly, he usually had a contract with his employer which helped him to increase his income; his vermin diary. In it he kept a meticulous record of every single crow and magpie, rat and hedgehog killed. He would submit the account and be paid a few pence for each one. The gibbet was the evidence; there, the corpses; in his diary, the tally. Thus could the accounts be audited.

Those few pence for his vermin did precious little for his income. To make pence into pounds, he would skin many of the animals he killed; the badgers, the foxes and sometimes the otters. There was, and still is to this day, a market for skins, and all he had to do, perhaps still does, was to wrap the skin up in a parcel and despatch it to the firm known as the gamekeeper's friend. Back would come by return the postal orders in payment, together with paper, string and printed labels ready for his next consignment. Maybe next time he would send a few stoat skins or a parcel of jay wings, with those blue and white striped feathers, that were so popular with the milliner.

Keepering had always worked by its inbuilt incentive system. There seemed no reason to change it, the ideas were handed down from father to son through the generations. They were just as glad of the perks from vermin, as they were of the handout from well satisfied sportsmen at the end of a day's shooting.

Producing that satisfaction was a long and weary struggle. Just consider those three thousand eggs that arrive on his doorstep one spring morning from the game farm. Knowing their arrival date, your gamekeeper has made preparations, making up nests in sitting boxes enclosed in a fox- and rat-proof pen. Next, he must find broody hens. This means a visit to every farm, small holding and cottage in the district where poultry are kept. After a lot of watchful haggling with farmers, honest and not so honest, he comes away with the 150 hens that he needs. Tests with dummy eggs precede a full month of brooding for the hens, and ceaseless vigilance for the keeper.

Every morning and evening, he takes the sitting hens off their nests, attaching them to a small stake by a slip of string on one leg. He gives them plenty of corn and water, and does not put them back on the nest, until each one has produced a neat pile of evidence that her previous meals have passed through her body. The keeper watches for signs of constipation. This could mean the eggs in her nest getting cold, and, eventually, a poor hatch from that clutch of eggs. One or two hens stand up on the job and must be replaced by more maternal birds. Some eggs get broken by clumsy hens. Apart from these pre-hatching problems, he has to expect some stale or infertile eggs, and, in the last days, his anxious touch tells him which those are. At long last the chicks hatch, and as he counts, the casualties of weather or clumsy hens increase before his eyes.

During the month-long wait for the eggs to hatch, the keeper has prepared the next stage of the operation. A fairly flat, but well drained field has been earmarked, or, if necessary, hired. This field, which would otherwise have yielded a crop of hay, now holds the creosoted coops in which the surviving chicks will live out the next few weeks. It is then that the long days really begin; feeding, watering, moving coops to a fresh square. During this time, the keeper often lives in his cabin on the field, ready to act should a sudden storm start flood pools, or an inquisitive fox or cat come prowling around.

If the chicks survive these hazards, as well as the attentions of sparrow hawk, rat and stoat and the rigours of disease, then, when they begin to grow feathers, coops, hens and chicks are moved to cover. Life gets a little easier for the keeper at this stage, but the constant round of feeding continues, as does his vigilance against predators. Once the pheasants have outgrown their coops, and begin to roost, the presence of a fox actually can help in a curious way. With a fox about, the pheasants are quickly persuaded that a roost in the trees is safer than one on the ground, where they would otherwise rest quite happily.

Eventually October arrives, the shooting season starts, though not in earnest, and the task, of rearing at least, is over. A few months later gamekeeper and landlord can do their sums, working out how many pheasants from the 3000 eggs fell to the gun. Sometimes it is only half, or even a third, of the egg batch.

It is small wonder then, that the keeper had to work around the clock against vermin, trespassers and poachers, his three enemies.

43

To do his job properly he had to be clever, as well as industrious; never being in the same place at the same time each day, always varying his routine like any present-day carrier of bullion. He used cover to move from point to point like a military patrol, he was quiet, unobtrusive and, like the village policeman, a lonely man. For both of them a drink in a pub while on the beat was impossible.

Today things have changed. Incubators do the initial work on the eggs, heating lamps replace the broody hens, and, from the moment of hatching almost until the day of shooting, the pheasants are penned, safe from predators. Thankfully too, the attitudes in most cases towards predators have changed. Now we realise that by killing off every single crow, magpie, jay and fox in a given area, we merely make room for more to move in.

It was, perhaps, the unkeepered estates of wartime days that proved the point. After five years of no vermin control, there was still, in most areas, a plentiful supply of wild pheasants. What the prewar keeper was doing of course, was trying to beat the system. Pheasants like so many other species that lay large clutches of eggs or have large litters, have a high mortality rate among immature birds. Watch a hen pheasant in the wild—within a few days of hatching her eggs she may have half a dozen chicks, a week later only two or three. So the system was wrong, not the keeper. He was being asked to achieve the impossible, and in his battle against the balance of nature, he tipped the scales in favour of the game birds.

Undoubtedly, there are still keepers for whom tradition dies hard. They still, often unnecessarily, kill off everything that isn't a game bird. Fortunately, this type is getting rarer and rarer, but, sadly, keepers themselves are decreasing in number.

So although we may curse the old-time keeper, we should, I think, thank as well, that quiet man patrolling his boundaries, counting the cost. His black labrador at his heels, his twelve bore under his arm, ever listening, ever looking—he is a man with a job to do, but he is, above all, a naturalist.

44

Old Charlie

It was late on Saturday evening. The city streets buzzed with home-going traffic, car doors slammed and revellers from the pub across the way shouted their fond farewells. Bedtime. A last look round before retiring, a glance out of the first floor windows to the gardens and lawn below to make sure none of the late drinkers had decided to take home a floral peace offering from the flower beds.

All was well. There was not a soul in sight, except a solitary fox. There it was on the lawn below, a long lank and thin looking creature, sniffing around the grass, obviously nibbling something, occasionally pricking its ears nervously then dashing to the shadows, only to return a few seconds later to continue the forage for whatever food it was finding. There it stayed for a full hour with the city at its noisiest, while I watched from a darkened room. It was patently a nervous fox, but nonetheless, a fox at terms with life in a busy city.

It acted like a vixen, particularly a vixen which had spent spring

45

and early summer feeding a litter of cubs; for it was thin, with a poor coat, yet this couldn't be a vixen with such a long brush. This was a lean and hungry dog fox, a semi-detached surburban fox. It's not uncommon to see them roaming the streets in the early morning, keeping the milkman or the paper delivery boy company. Indeed, our paper used to be delivered by an elderly man who frequently met a fox on his early morning rounds, sitting on a gatepost, cleaning up. It's a strange feeling to see a fox dashing across the road in front of your car at 5 a.m. of a summer morning, yet these days you're more likely to see a fox in town than you are in the country.

Outside the town, foxes take advantage of the natural cover in woodland, pasture and hedgerow, but in the town they have to break cover to reach their resting place for the day. More and more foxes are finding that the pickings are easier in towns. Perhaps it's something to do with modern poultry farming practice, since fewer and fewer poultry are kept free-range. There just aren't so many of those rickety old henhouses that are such easy meat for a determined fox. And, after all, why should a fox risk a country fowl-run when, in the town, dustbins are full of edible rubbish, edible at least to a fox? A quick flick of the dustbin lid with hardly a sound (most lids are plastic these days anyway) and there's a meal fit for a king-fox. As for those bags that some councils provide for household rubbish, the contents come spilling out once a fox has torn a hole in the plastic or the paper.

Unfortunately for him my fox had come round a day too late, he'd missed the bus, or rather the lorry. The refuse collection men had been round the day before and the bins were empty. Not a plastic bag of smelly bones was to be had anywhere. So he had to resort to the lawns for, although foxes are generally thought of as carnivores, they are quite omnivorous in their eating habits. An examination of their droppings will show that even blackberries figure in their diet during the later months of the year. It has been suggested that foxes come into the towns and cities just for the night, but there's more and more evidence to suggest that they not

46

only live in and around towns, but breed there as well. Litters of cubs have been found under a railway signal box close to a city station, and people living in rambling Georgian houses have heard scuffles and squeaks in their cellars, again coming from a litter of cubs.

But, despite the evidence of my own eyes, the morning after my meeting with that town fox, I had to take a good look around the garden. It wasn't that I had disbelieved my own eyes but rather that I wanted some concrete evidence of exactly what that fox had been finding to eat on the lawn. Had it been snails, of which that garden had more than enough, I would have expected to find bits of broken shells littered around. A long hard search gave not a clue, and I can only conclude that worms made the fox's meal that night. But if I wanted confirmation that I hadn't been dreaming, I found that in one corner of the garden; nothing material, just a sudden whiff in the breeze of that pungent foxy smell, where the animal had left his mark on a tussock of grass. Yes, my fly-by-night fox had been there alright.

Tally Ho and All That

Arguing the pro and cons of blood sports like hunting is best left to those who do the hunting. It can certainly not be argued that fox hunting controls the fox population. Indeed, were it not for fox hunts, foxes might soon become an extinct species, since other more efficient means of controlling foxes would be more widely used. While some hill farmers would perhaps welcome that state of affairs, it would be yet another piece missing from the jigsaw puzzle that makes up the overall balance of nature.

For my own part, I've followed many a hunt on foot, bike or by motor car, and, for the most part, enjoyed the day out. That I think, is the definition, from the countryman's point of view, that gives some justification for the sport—a day out. For farmer and farm worker, it provides a chance to get away from the round of work that for many of them takes seven days a week, a chance to meet neighbours, maybe to do a bit of bartering business. It is a social gathering, and often achieves much more than the infrequent meeting of the parish council. For the countryman it is the equivalent of a visit to the theatre.

Hunting folk have a language all their own. The ceremonial begins with the 'meet', the coming together of the main participants. However, at this stage in the best hunting circles, one of the principals is missing—the fox. It has been whispered that in some hunts, the fox is also present at the meet, in a sack, ready to be released should there be a scarcity of foxes in the area. It is, however, just a whisper, and may safely be dismissed as idle gossip.

Some of the followers turn up at the meet already mounted on their horses. These mounts vary, from the elegant, well groomed hunter, the potential Grand National winner, through the many shapes and sizes of ponies down to the sort of scruffy horse that has patently only been caught that morning from a muddy field and would be more at home between the shafts of a cart than underneath the well-rounded figure of the farmer. Other horses though, arrive in state, and they have to be 'unboxed', although that word is hardly ever used. More often the order is heard to 'let the old sod out before he kicks the sides in'.

The hunt members, while all this is going on, greet each other with great good humour, saving their politest greetings for one man who gets the courteous address 'Good morning, master'. This is not the head of the local school who has also taken the day off, like so many others in the village, but a very important person indeed. He is the master of fox hounds, the MFH, and some of these gentlemen not only carry those letters after their name, but even manage to obtain a registration number for their car with those same letters.

After the horses, the animals next in descending order of size at the meet are the hounds. These are known collectively as the pack, and such is the well ordered life of hunting that on one meet the master will be hunting a dog pack, and the following meet, a bitch pack. In this way he manages to keep the hounds' minds on the job in hand, hunting foxes.

The hounds—and never call them dogs in front of hunting

people—are under the direct control of the huntsman and the whipper-in. The fact that the master may also be the huntsman, only adds to the confusion of the outsider. Suffice it to say that the master and huntsman between them control the way the day's hunting will be conducted. The whipper-in looks after the hounds and makes sure he ends the day with the same number that he started with. These two, huntsman and whip, know every single member of the pack by name, even though they all look exactly alike. This similarity in itself is not surprising, since they have probably all been bred from a very particular strain, and that is born out in their names: Lancier, Lancelot, Leander and so on. Names beginning with the same letter often indicate that they've come from the same litter.

If you should feel moved to show your perspicacity and remark to any of the hunt officials that you notice he has twenty five hounds out with him today, don't be surprised if his idea of arithmetic and yours are at variance. In hunting terms his hounds number twelve and a half couple—just another of their idiosyncracies. Then there's the business of those red coats. It's known as hunting pink, even though in some cases it may not be pink or red at all, but green, even yellow. Huntin' is so confusin'.

Fortunately meets often occur at pubs, which means that while the hunt members are entertained to a drink, the stirrup cup, the rest of us who happen to be around, can have one as well, with the slight disadvantage that we have to pay for ours.

On the subject of paying, there is one other slight ceremony that will occur before the hunt moves off to the business of the day. There will almost certainly be someone around who, if he or she doesn't actually say 'alms for the love of Allah', expresses very much that idea by the cap-in-hand approach. This is known logically enough, as 'the cap', and in it one is expected to deposit a coin of the realm, preferably this realm. This is your contribution or entrance fee to the day's sport. There is, however, a way around this that some people use, people who are as crafty as the fox who is supposed to lead everyone a jolly dance during the day. To save money there are those who join late, often with the excuse that a cow has calved, or granny has had another of her turns.

At long last the hunting day gets under way, with the first draw. That's another term they use, and all it means is that the hounds are encouraged to investigate the possibilities of Farmer Bailey's five acre patch of kale, or Squire's home plantation. If fox there be, the pack soon let everyone know by 'giving tongue' and to many countrymen it's the most exciting sound there is. First one hound whimpers as it catches the scent of a fox, soon to be followed by two or three more, until the whole pack gets on the line and the noise becomes a spine-chilling, echoing symphony. There's not much else to learn. If you don't know the country that's just about the last you'll see of the hunt all day.

On the other hand, if you know your local geography, and have taken notice of the wind direction, you can set yourself up in a few well chosen vantage points. That way you'll see more activity, and probably more foxes, than any of the followers on horseback. But, beware. Finding a good spot to see the hunt, and getting all excited at seeing that fox, can lead to the master expressing very strong disapproval in language that is more than likely to be somewhat flowery. Putting the fox off it's chosen path once it has broken cover is a sin without parallel in hunting circles. 'Heading the fox' has often led to a member of the hunt being sent home with a well-worded flea in his ear from the irate master.

Here are some final words of warning. The fox doesn't have a face, but a 'mask'; not a tail, but a 'brush'; not a foot, but a 'pad'. If you happen to see that fox loping away along a farm hedge, while the hounds and the master and his staff are fiddling about on the other side of the valley some two miles behind the fox, there is a right and wrong way to inform the hunt. The traditional way is, 'View, halloo!' and not, 'There the little bugger goes!'.

Good hunting.

The Cuckoo Dove

The song of the nightingale is one of the most beautiful sounds of our countryside. Most of us would go a hundred miles or more just to take a sip of that summer wine. Unhappily, most of us may have to soon since the sort of habitat needed by the bird—the hazel coppices regularly harvested for sheep fencing—is being eroded, eaten away. Not that the bird has always had such a place in my affections. Indeed not so many years ago, it led to a month of sleepless nights, and listless days punctuated by explosions of the sort of language to bring blushes at the vicar's tea party.

A nightingale singing its song the night through, right outside the bedroom window, can only be compared with a pneumatic drill, or a factory production line in its effect on one's nervous system and sleeping habits. However, I'd gladly swap that bird for the one that threatens all of our resting hours. It hasn't been with us for much more than twenty years, yet, in that short time, it has replaced the farmyard rooster as the proclaimer of the dawn, and, whereas the cockerel used to be very much the countryside's factory hooter, this bird, the collared dove, calls in town and country alike.

Of all the raucous, boring sounds made by any of our native birds, the 'song' of the collared dove takes some beating. It's a dull repetitive call of three notes that any musician would discard, a flat, monotony of 'coo-coo-cuk', repeated time and time again,

interpersed with a shriek that sounds like a tom cat expressing disapproval of the effects of a well aimed boot. What a strange contrast it is, because it is quite a beautiful bird in appearance, looking like a small pigeon with a rather grey oystershell plumage, and a distinctive black and white 'back to front' collar. If only elegance were proportional to song, the collared dove should have been the lead treble of the church choir. As it is, it's the failed soprano.

Its persistence in song, however, is reflected in the adaptability of the bird. At the turn of this century, it is generally reckoned that the collared dove's only foothold in Europe was in the Balkans, and it was unknown in the British Isles until the mid fifties, when the first pair supposedly bred in Norfolk. Yet twenty years later, it is rapidly becoming one of our commonest birds. It's moved in on us—and has made its presence felt, or rather heard. Nor has it confined its explosions to the mainland. I sat in a cosy bar in Jersey, looking out on to the chestnut trees in the Royal Square of St. Helier, not so very long ago, and counted not just one but twenty-four of the birds. They were, it seemed, rapidly taking over the trees and ledges of the Square from the feral pigeons that for so long had ruled that particular roost.

The speed of their spread through the country must also be in direct proportion to their breeding habits. I had one nest under observation for a couple of days, and was hatching great plans to stick a microphone underneath when the young burst from the eggs, and so get some unique recordings. Perhaps 'nest' is a flattery, it was a platform of haphazard twigs resting precariously across a slender fork of the tree, so small that the parent bird's fore and aft were clearly visible over the edges of the nest. But when I thought the time was ripe to set up the recording equipment, I saw on the lawn one morning a parent collared dove and her single young one, almost as perfectly marked as the mature bird. Then, a few days later, the boring calling started up again in the trees, and the mating and breeding cycle was off once again.

The collared dove has one other claim to fame. Not a year goes by without the country's newspapers cooing on about 'hearing the first cuckoo in spring.' It's a pastime without which the correspondence columns would seem dull. These letters give a breath of the true realities of life, sprinkled as they are among the far away topics of international problems. During 1974, it was in late January that the first letters appeared claiming to have heard the first cuckoo of the year. One gentleman enquired if his hearing the bird was a record, and the rejoinder a few days later reassured him that indeed it was a record—made by Ludwig Koch!

Undoubtedly, in these days of the small cassette recording machine, some of the blame for these phoney first cuckoos is being placed firmly where it belongs, at the door of the prankster with a machine. Let us not forget either the ability of many a small boy to reproduce the call of the cuckoo by his own vocal agility.

At long last, however, I think we have nailed the real culprit, the bird that is not the first cuckoo at all, but the bird that is spreading through the country like a grey bush fire. It is, of course, the collared dove, whose boring triple note is not dissimilar to the double note of the cuckoo. In certain circumstances the two birds could be confused, particularly if a pair of collared doves should be calling, one against the other. After all we have to resort to a sort of cuckoo language to describe the collared doves' call. 'Coo-coo-cuk, Coo-Coo-Cuk.'

What will the correspondence columns of the newspapers do now?

Old Man of the Woods

Four weary travellers were working on a small island in the middle of Loch Lomond, on the sort of day when rain started pouring out of the leaden skies at an early hour and gave every indication of filling the loch to overflowing in record time. Even by Scottish standards it was wet, and so were we, the weary travellers. As we descended from the higher parts of the island down to the shore, we noticed the pungent smell of wood-smoke in the air, and, down by the shore, we came upon a pile of driftwood smouldering sulkily in the rain. Close by crouched a flimsy square tent.

Our coming apparently hadn't gone unnoticed; from out of the tent, there appeared a small wizened figure of a man. His clothes seemed hardly fit to keep out the weather, but we realised after a second glance that he was at that particular moment far better equipped than the four people at his doorstep. We were invited inside, and there he had a sleeping bag, tins of food and, above all, a pot of steaming, smokey tea. He insisted on sharing it, hospitality one would never expect in such remote parts.

The man, however, was not a total recluse. Apparently, he spent every summer there on the lochside; making occasional trips back to so called civilisation, rowing his flimsy boat across the loch, and staying just long enough to collect a few pounds of Social Security, a few more supplies. Why he chooses this way of seeing the summer through we didn't ask. When you are receiving a man's hospitality, you may intrude on the privacy of his property, but not on the privacy of his mind. Clearly, he was supremely happy alone, very nearly cut off from his fellow men; a loner, but a part-timer. Come the hard winter, he would be back in a Glasgow tenement, longing for the days of spring when he could return to the loch.

Other men go the whole hog, finding, even in our own countryside, the sort of solitude associated with desert islands, and living in the sort of conditions that only an island can provide. They find themselves a little paradise in a wood or forest, living in a tent or more often a sort of shack they've made themselves from the general clutter of the countryside. Some of them have no contact at all with the world around them, others make fleeting journeys back to our way of life, but these are only brief flirtations to collect what food they can't provide from their own kingdom. These are the old men of the woods.

The woodsman I know, or at least the woodsman with whom I have become acquainted, for no-one ever really knows this kind of man, is tall with a prominent nose. He has an aggressive chin and finely chiselled features, sculpted by the winds of the world and the salt of the seven seas. He too came from Scotland, and at the age of twelve ran away from school to sea.

It's the traditional start to a story of success enjoyed by many a youngster, unhappy with his lot. Running away to sea in those days meant, for this man, sailing before the mast on the run to Murmansk, and there can't be a much tougher apprenticeship. If that was tough, his next port of call, 'the old Foreign Legion in 1912', was even tougher. He dismisses it as if it were common for a lad to join the French desert forces. 'Got out of that in September

'14, came back to this country to join the Army. The Army wouldn't have us.'

He went back to the sea in the Merchant Service, and was torpedoed three or four times. He then joined the Royal Navy, and, for the last years of the war, was on the North Sea patrols from Scapa to Rosyth.

After World War 1, America, that land of great opportunities beckoned, because 'there wasn't much work here'. Urban America, like other large centres, may have been paved with gold, but these weren't the roads that this loner wished to walk. They were not for him, but the border countries were, and there the woodsman in him emerged.

Lumber camps in Wyoming, Columbia and the Rockies gave him the solitude that he needed. This didn't last long; 'I didn't care for the French Canadians a great deal.' The company of his fellow men was not for him, except for those shipmates aboard a ship bound for Australia. There he fared little better than in America, and, after a further six months in New Zealand, with all the casualness of a man boarding a bus to nowhere in particular, he fetched up in Mombasa.

In Africa, he became involved with white hunters. 'We were on the elephants for a time, and then the licences came on, and that put paid, and then I started to run transport.' He trots out the information reluctantly, without embellishment, assuming that what he did could have been done by anyone. In a sense it could have been, by a man with his tenacity of purpose. Running transport in Africa turned out to be a continent-wide enterprise; 'down from Abysinia and Somaliland, down then through Kenya over to the Congo and Tanganyika and Salisbury, Rhodesia.' He might have been saying that he took a bus trip to Blackpool. But going to Blackpool, you don't end up with malaria and blackwater fever, which is what his African adventure cost him. Despite this, one detects regret in his voice that he can't go back to the tropics again.

His philosophy in life has been simple. 'You just go about, and some things just happen. That's the way life is. If you go looking for a thing you'll never find it. The time when you find it is when you're not looking.' His is a philosophy that has served him well, but although, in a way, he has become a true philosopher, he denies that he has the knowledge to deserve this title.

'My father always used to drum into us the fact that "if you talk you can't listen, if you don't listen you don't learn".' Today he confesses that he's only just starting to learn, but confines himself to those things that he can get his teeth into. 'To learn anything you've got to get down to the foundations and build up.' He adds laconically that, 'to understand the English language, you've got to understand the classics.'

This comes from a man who ran away from school at the age of twelve, and today is in his eighty-first year, finding tremendous pleasure in living his lonely life, comforted by woodland creatures, woodland flowers, and his garden. There, he grows roses with not a blemish on them. His vegetable patch keeps him busy and also keeps him provided.

The man is an enigma. There is so much to his story, but because he is the sort of man not given easily to telling that story, one must accept it without question. I don't even know his surname. I've never asked, he's never volunteered the information.

These days, the confidences we pass are those about the wildlife of the woods; the arrival of the first migrant birds, the first nests, the butterflies, the badgers and the foxes. He shuns the companionship of man, choosing rather his fellow creatures of the wood. Perhaps there is one regret in his life, apart from not being able to go back to Africa, and this concerns the frailty of age. It's a small matter, more of an annoyance than a cause for real regret; he finds that he can no longer hear the grasshopper warblers.

No Time to Stand and Stare

We've gone nature trail mad in some parts of the country. Some are excellently organised, particularly the designated reserves watched over by responsible national bodies. However modest woodland rides have suddenly become graced with the grand name of nature trail; industry and big business are seen to be making a token gesture to the spirit of conservation by sponsoring trails and putting up notices to remind us of their concern.

Some of these so-called trails, though, are of very little value. They are trodden by hundreds of parties every single day, dogs and prams in tow, making enough noise to waken the sleepiest dormouse. The trees are bare of bird life and lower branches too, as eager passers-by grab a twig to use as a fly-swish. There is not an animal to be seen, not even a frightened rabbit. In such conditions the hopes of seeing very much, except perhaps a grey squirrel attracted in by our rubbish, are practically nil.

These trails have a marginal value in introducing schoolchildren to some tree and plant species, but that's about all. In time too, the path which has suddenly become a nature trail, is a path no more. It can't stand the pressure of thousands of walking feet. It becomes potholed and muddy in one season, and a dust-choked nightmare in another.

This is the only real value of this pseudo nature trail; it channels us, the inquisitives, along set routes. It stops us wandering all over the place, and contains the damage that we do to one particular stretch of woodland or park.

In this way it controls the erosion of the countryside that is increasing every year as more and more remote parts are brought, by the network of motorways, within easier and easier reach of millions more people. If, indeed, these paths have to be called 'nature trails' in order to make us walk them in the forlorn hope of seeing something interesting, then they at least serve a purpose.

There are several golden rules to observe if we are to get the greatest possible pleasure out of a country walk. Let's take clothing first of all, and since walking is our object, the feet have the most important part to play. Dry feet are essential, and that means stout shoes or boots, but far better I think, are the good old faithful wellingtons. They stand less chance of taking in water, should you happen to put your foot in a stream that is deeper than you think. They prevent the calves getting stung by nettles or scratched by brambles. But in the choice of wellingtons, beware. Those smooth-soled lightweight ones may be all right for pottering in the garden, but they are dangerous on a country walk. They offer no grip at all on a steep and slippery path, and could lead to a badly strained back.

A pair of wellingtons with good patterned soles is what you want, and a pair that fits snugly around the legs. Just take a few steps in wellingtons that flap against the calves as you walk. The noise is like a heavily amplified metronome, and that's going to scare any wildlife away long before you get within sight. So make sure the wellingtons fit properly, and if they are noisy, wear sea-boot stockings and turn them, fisherman-fashion, over the tops of the boots. That way you deaden the noise and keep out twigs and thorns.

There are ways and ways of walking. Tip-toeing is hopeless. This transfers the body weight onto a smaller area of foot, thus increasing the pressure exerted over the area of contact. Besides which, it makes the legs ache. Feet flat down all the time means less chance of snapping twigs, and, this way, it's also possible to feel a twig, and if it starts to give, to ease off before it breaks. Walking silently is easy with a little practice, and once mastered is half the battle of getting really close to life in the wild.

As for the colour of clothing, that isn't really important. The man who goes out with a complete camouflage outfit has wasted his money. He can wear a bright red cloak, but the bull in the field won't even notice it because it is colour blind. It's much more likely to react to the sterling silver of his watch strap, or the glass on the dial reflecting flashes of sunlight like a semaphore signal.

The real treasures of the countryside are most often seen by the man who, having taken his walk, stands and stares quietly in one place, not shuffling his feet, breathing quietly, and keeping even his eye movements slow and deliberate. It is useless to try and make out that you are part of a tree by sticking behind a tree trunk and peeping round it now and again. If there's a roe deer or a fox in front of you, the moment your nose comes round the trunk, it will be away in a flash.

Talking of noses, remember that the sense of smell in many animals comes a pretty close second to their sense of sight. If you're standing and looking, it's no use at all having the wind blowing from behind you, that only carries your smell towards whatever may be about. Face the breeze always.

Always use natural cover, like a small thicket of birch saplings or anything that will break up your outline, but there's certainly no need to festoon your hat with pieces of bracken or greenery. All movements should be slow and deliberate; standing still needs patience, but that patience is invariably rewarded. Wildlife that scuttled to cover when you arrived will very soon be out and about when you've settled down. Often this happens surprisingly quickly. A rustle of leaves, a movement in the trees above your head will be the first signs, but don't try and take a look straight away. By remaining still, whatever it was that moved will move again, and usually closer to you.

I've sat still, deep in a woodland, and seen the tiny movements of very small birds high in the canopy above. Because I didn't know exactly what they were, I just stayed where I was, doing absolutely nothing. Within three minutes those birds had come lower and lower, until a pair of them flitted in a small bush not two feet from me, to be joined by the rest of the flock. There they were, these goldcrests, bowing their heads to show the brilliant golden flash. Birds are always on the move, but because I just sat there, they came close. Had I moved, they would have stayed high in the treetops.

A walk alone is the most rewarding, but if it must be more than a solo, selfish ramble, your companion should be someone with whom you've worked out an understanding. When you stop, he or she stops instantly, even if it means standing precariously on one leg for a few seconds. There must be no conversation or pointing. There's no need for either, just follow the other's glance, and you'll soon pick up what he or she has spotted.

There it is, then, a few basic lessons in country craft, and if you want to learn more, go out with a real countryman. The man may be leading you round a bend in a woodland path, and will suddenly freeze and expect you to do the same. He'll beckon you to his side with a movement of his eyes, and there, loping away from you is a dog fox. The fact that you've managed to get so close to it is a sure sign that you've learned some of the country craft.

Then you may get another lesson. Your guide will place the back of his hand against his lips and produce a noise like a rabbit screaming when it is being attacked by a stoat. He might, this country companion, even show you how to hoot a tawny owl down from a tree to fly so close to you that you can feel the rush of air as it 'buzzes' you. If you're lucky he might even show you special places that he and he alone knows.

Follow his example, and you too can become a country craftsman, and you too will find special places, places to be shared eventually only with special people. Some of the secrets of the countryside will be yours. Some, not all—for that would take more than a lifetime of standing and staring.

Fit for a King

Gastronomic memories live on with me longer than most other memories. Be it a pub lunch of bread and cheese, washed down with a quart of real farmhouse cider, or a slightly false medieval banquet set in an Irish castle for the benefit of American tourists, I'll remember.

But there's one meal that I cherish more than any other, and I can still remember the flavour now, some years after. It was basic, it was simple and the preparation may not have met with the approval of Fanny Craddock, but then who needs all those sauces and an assistant chef to make a meal to remember? This meal needed only a brace of trout from the stream, a blazing wood fire, a frying pan and a little butter. Of course, no true countryman is ever without his pocket knife; it doesn't have to be the sort that will remove boy scouts from horses' hooves, just a simple two-bladed affair of good steel. Given that, anyone can scrape the scales from the trout and clean it, and then use the same implement to turn the fish in the pan, and spear the fish when cooked.

It may not be elegant, but, with a meal like that—fresh fish that falls apart at the touch, spiced by the smoke from the wood fire —who cares about the finer points of table manners? The flavour of that meal could never be reproduced by even the cordon bleu chefs of high cuisine.

The fact is that many countrymen themselves don't realise just how much they rely on the true wild produce of their environment to supplement the supermarket foods of today. There was a time when many a country-cottager would expect to have fresh rabbit on his menu once a week, a rabbit caught in the field at the end of the garden or, even more likely, in the garden itself.

Setting up the snare for the rabbit is quite straightforward. A home-made loop of wire is attached by strong cord to a small stake driven into the ground. The snare is held off the ground by a short, split stick in the split end of which the noose rests. All that is simple enough. The secret is in knowing where to set the snare.

Rabbits, being very much creatures of habit, follow well defined runs to their feeding grounds. These runs are easy to spot and the snare must be set in a run so that the rabbit will stick its head through the noose! Just anywhere along the run will not do. It must not be placed too close to the hedge because rabbits are cautious, and invariably have a good look round on emerging from the undergrowth. Equally, it's not much use putting the snare at the far end of the run where the rabbit will be chewing up the grass and its movements will only be short and hesitant.

The chosen spot must be where the animal has put on speed, somewhere between the two points, and even this choice is critical. By careful examination of the ground, it's possible to see that the rabbit puts its feet down at just about the same point on every journey in a series of hops. To ensure 90 per cent success, the snare should be placed half way between a take-off point and a landing point. The 10 per cent error is for two eventualities: the snare may be set with too wide a noose, which the rabbit can dive through like a circus performer; the noose may, on the other hand, be too narrow, and will simply be brushed aside by the passing rabbit.

These days of course, the rabbit has disappeared from many a table because of myxomatosis. It's not that there's any chance of contracting the ghastly disease, but the sight of a rabbit in its death-throes can upset the stomach of even the most hardened countryman. There are ways of catching game birds, to provide a right royal meal instead. I don't want to increase the number of poachers in the country, or to give away the secrets of others who are tolerated because they take only for their own needs and not for financial gain. Suffice it to say that one doesn't need a shot-gun, and even a rabbit snare, suitably adapted, will do the trick.

Of course, some 'spoils' are perfectly legitimate. Many pheasants come to grief against the radiator grills of motor vehicles. One such bird still made very good eating, after a motorist had suffered the collision, and was in some distress at the sight of a fluttering and injured bird. The motorist behind took the matter, and the bird, out of the chap's hands!

For some collisions though, a really substantial vehicle is necessary. There was, some years ago, a well built and solid army staff-car known as the Humber '4 by 4'. One night in North Germany, one of my colleagues was returning to base in the faithful Humber, and happened to collide with a large wild boar. There was not a dent in the car. The boar was dead and, after veterinary examination, provided the mess with a very welcome addition to the usual bill of fare.

Those are a few instances of high-living off the land, but they can be supplemented by other delicacies. A patch of wild strawberries, bearing fruit the size of good round garden peas, is well worth knowing about, and keeping to yourself. A plateful may take a little time in the picking, but, once gathered and covered with a sprinkling of sugar and cream, tastes just as good as the cultivated variety. I've even known some people who make jam from the wild strawberry, which, apart from the size of the fruit, is indistinguishable from the other kind. Besides which I understand, from those who have trouble setting strawberry jam made from the bigger fruits, that there's never any problem with the wild fruits.

Wild strawberries and raspberries may make delicious jam, but, for sumptious, luscious fruit-tarts, there is only one ingredient for my money. The picking poses a problem. These fruits grow in remote parts, up in the hills, and they grow so close to the ground that a backache is inevitable, as are purple-stained fingers. It's slow work, too. You can be stooping there, harried by flies and eaten by midges for all of an hour, and you'll hardly have enough to cover the bottom of a basket. This tiny, troublesome, but delicious fruit goes by a variety of names. In Radnorshire they are called whim-berries, elsewhere wortleberries, bilberries or blaeberries. Call it what you will, put them in a pie and I'll be happy to put them in my stomach.

Picking berries can, as everyone knows, be a messy business but hands can get stained, too, from walnuts, and, as I write, my hands show all the evidence of preparing walnuts for pickling. Walnuts are pretty rare these days. The timber of the tree is so valuable that few owners can resist the high prices offered them by timber merchants. Such financial inducements are difficult to ignore. Money in the bank now is a better prospect than collecting walnuts maybe every other year when the tree actually bears fruit. Even then it can be a race between the owner of the tree and the squirrels, of both the two and four-legged variety!

Storing nuts is usually a matter of personal preference, but when it comes to walnuts my favourite method is to place them in a large box in layers, covering each layer with dry sand and a sprinkle of salt. Come Christmas, you will know the real meaning of 'sweet as a nut': Sadly though, the times when we could look to a box the size of a tea chest full of those delicious nuts have gone, with the trees that bore the nuts.

The hazel-nut is another nut worth the trouble of collecting and storing. One old country way of keeping those moist is to place them in a seven pound biscuit tin and bury the lot in the garden, carefully marking the spot of course! Sweet chestnuts, those beautiful moist, crisp nuts, may be picked for nothing but a very little labour. Who needs to buy expensive bags of mixed nuts when the festive season comes around? The countryside is indeed a great garden if only one knows what to look for, and when to look.

Nowadays it's quite the vogue to make table wines, both sparkling or still, with the aid of all the basic ingredients, including glass tubes and corks bought as a DIY pack. The real countryman can make wine from practically anything growing, and he doesn't need U-tubes and thermometers to do it. The fruits of the field are the essentials, along with some baker's yeast and a large stone crock. Mind you, there can be some nasty explosions from bottles corked down before the wine has finished working, but it's a welcome sound, a sound full of promise. Wheat and potato wine can be made, both with a kick like a highland mule, and the nearest thing to scotch whisky I've ever tried. Parsnip wine, dandelion wine, cowslip wine, each has its individual flavour and colour. Elderberry wine can be as good as burgundy, and, for a warming drink of a cold winter morning, there's nothing better than sloe gin.

Happy indeed is the man who can reap such fruits from the natural harvest of the fields and hedges.

Small Bird, Big Tree

We don't seem to plant trees for posterity these days, not in the way our ancestors did. On the face of it the decision they made —to lay out their parklands with timber from many parts of the world—was an act without any self-interest; for the owners could never gain the benefit of their expensive planting in their own lifetime. The real reason must lie in the fact that it was fashionable to landscape one's property, to lay it out with exotic trees and shrubs. Each man vied with the next door neighbour, to have an estate with, if not the magic touch of Capability Brown about it, then at least the next best thing.

Their undertakings cost perhaps a thousand pounds in the early 1800s for seedlings which were often raised from seeds imported from the colonies. These trees are the legacy we have all inherited, particularly in the case of estates that have passed from a long family line to the hands of the National Trust, the Forestry Commission or a local authority.

It's not hard to imagine the awe felt by the early travellers on catching their first glimpse of the 'big tree' of California and the visions they had of those same trees growing in England. When they saw them though, these giant sequoias were already thousands of years old. The world's largest tree (not the tallest) is reckoned to be a sequoia. This is the General Sherman in the Sequoia National Park in central California, a giant, two hundred and seventy-two feet tall, one hundred and one feet around the base of its trunk, and maybe three and a half thousand years old. It was natural then, that sequoias from the slopes of the Sierra Nevada should be introduced to the lowlier altitudes of English parklands for, although we shall probably never have a specimen to vie with General Sherman, they add elegance and majesty to the oak, beech, ash and elm.

The first seeds of the sequoia were brought over in 1853 and so, to-day the examples in our parks are, at most, only one hundred and twenty years old. The Cherokee Indian name has all but been forgotten in England. At the time of their introduction the hero of the country, the Duke of Wellington, had died the previous year. In his honour the trees were named wellingtonias.

The bark of the wellingtonia soft, spongy and thick, is a built-in protection against fire in its native habitat. Apart from the reddish brown bark which 'gives' at the pressure of the thumb, they are remarkable trees in another way, because they provide us with evidence of a startling piece of adaptation happening in our own time.

Any wellingtonia is well worth examining closely, particularly around the trunk at about head height. Often one can see tiny rivulets, a dirty white in colour, rather like the trace of resin flowing from a broken larch limb. This, though, is not a natural juice from the tree itself, but the droppings of a small bird. Just above the stain marks there will be a neatly chiselled hole not much bigger than a pigeon's egg, finely shaped, an avian work of art. This is not vandalism in the bird world, but a tiny bird taking legitimate advantage of the tree's soft bark.

The bird in question, the treecreeper is shy and not easy to see as

73

it darts up the tree-trunk investigating every nook and cranny for insects and larvae. Its dark brown upper plumage merges into the background, yet the holes it makes and the droppings it leaves on the wellingtonias are a sure sign that treecreepers are around. These small excavations in the soft bark are the roosting holes of the bird, just big enough for it to tuck its body inside, its stiff tail out. Once again, it is perfectly camouflaged, since the whiteness of its breast is hidden away. These birds do occur of course, in areas of the country where there are no specimens of this grand tree, and then the winter roost is behind bits of loose bark, or in natural holes left by a fallen branch.

Wellingtonias have only been in England for little more than a century, and it is not until the tree has been growing for maybe half that time that the bark would be thick enough to accommodate the treecreeper. So in something like sixty years at the most, one of our native birds has carved itself out a niche, and a cosy one at that.

Survival

Even the commoniest, dirtiest, scruffiest house sparrow is an object lesson in the art of survival. In terms of nuisance around the house, they are only surpassed by another of my least-loved birds, the starling. Both are the grand opportunists when it comes to nesting sites, finding a space under the tiles which would hardly let in a winter draught. Both too are much better adapted to living in our laps than most other species; they are always first at the bird table when in truth, we are trying to see the real garden birds through the colder months of the year with a supply of food. The sparrows, unfortunately, get the best of the pickings.

Perhaps though, their very acclimatisation to our environment has made them less wary than they should be. While working in the garden one day, I was aware of a motley collection of those sparrows near me. They were finding food at the other end of the bank on which I was working. But in the same moment that I noticed them their numbers declined by one. It was all over in a flash, and it was only when I saw the kestrel disappearing over the roof of the house trailing behind it a small shower of feathers, that I realised what had happened. This was one of the laws of nature in action—that only the fittest and the wariest survive.

In this field sparrows are absolute beginners, and the specialists are the blackbirds. Just watch them as they peck through the mulching around the rose bushes; the blackbird will take a few hops, throw the debris to one side, pause, cock an eye to the sky, and only then search for the elusive worm. It's a pattern that's repeated all the time that the bird is engaged in foraging for food. Even the slightest movement will send it scurrying for cover in the bushes or away to a vantage point on the rooftops. Blackbirds may have become garden birds in the course of time, but their woodland background and the innate survival reflexes are obvious.

Blackbirds once involved me in a most fascinating little drama that showed survival at work as well as the inter-relationship between predator and prey. In this case, like all good dramatic productions, there was also a secondary plot.

Deep in the wood, close to a gaunt oak covered with ivy, there was sudden and considerable activity among the blackbirds. First, one bird struck up with the key note, that 'snip-snipping' that is a warning call. Then it was joined by another bird, and then another, in a complete chorus that spelt danger. Every bird close to that oak was agitated. It is a sound that means only one thing—a characteristic collective battle between the blackbirds and a tawny owl, in which the smaller prey gang up on the larger predator and mob it.

I could see none of the protagonists, but if I had any doubts about the significance of the sounds, they were brushed aside by the faintest single hoot from the tawny owl somewhere in that oak tree. Then came the secondary plot; for I wasn't the only wanderer in the woods attracted by the unseen battle. Out of the corner of my eye I saw just the merest glimpse of a pair of pointed ears and a white-tipped tail disappearing into the undergrowth. A fox too, had been drawn to the battleground by the warning calls of the blackbirds; another opportunist was at work. With the departure of the fox, I made for the tree and brought the contest to an end; as I stood under the branches the tawny owl, in silent, graceful flight, disappeared.

It would, perhaps, be logical to assume that, the bigger the bird, the better the chances of survival, but it's a false assumption. It was only through the activities of a pair of crows flying in a most unlikely and haphazard formation with a great black-backed gull above a plantation of tall larches, that I discovered a heronry. Those two black killers and the arch scavenger were obviously interested in something in the tree-tops, and the magnet that was drawing them was, in fact, a group of herons' nests. As it transpired from the fracas in the heronry, there were some young in the nests, and I would suspect that the gull and the crows were drawn by the prospect of grabbing a heron chick.

One would have thought that the adult herons, large as they are, would be quite capable of seeing off the crows and the gull. The fact is that it would only take the combined efforts of both predator species to move the parent heron from the vicinity. Just a few yards would be enough, and then crow or gull would swoop and grab a chick. I'm not suggesting for one moment that this was a case of deliberate co-operation between the crows and the gull. It is far more likely that one or other had spotted those open nests high in the trees and moved in on the target, only to be joined by the second predator when the herons went into vocal dispute.

This was opportunism in action again, and it's only when you see an incident like this, that you realise just how vulnerable a heron's nest can be. It may look remote and well protected when we look at it from ground level, but seen from the air, it's like an inviting open larder, containing food for crows and gulls in the shape of eggs or young.

Many species rely on camouflage for protection, but just now and again, one sees an example of that other means of survival —speed coming into play. The young roe deer, the kid, is a beautiful example of self-preservation by camouflage. It can lie still for hours in a shady spot, with the sunlight playing through the leaves of the bushes and producing polka dot shadows on the ground. In those polka dots the speckled coat of the kid is well-nigh impossible to see. It's safe, and often left alone by the doe, while she feeds at the woodland edge. Walking through a sparse wood on a day when the sun was carpeting the ground with just such shadows, I approached a bank, not more than a couple of feet high. My approach, I like to think, was silent, and what breeze there was was blowing into my face. I was less than ten yards from that bank, with the sun and wind in my eyes, when a roe-deer doe jumped up just beyond the bank, and disappeared in double-quick time into a clump of rhododendrons beyond.

As she went from view, offering a fleeting vision of pricked ears and flashing white rump, there was a yap like a terrier giving tongue to a rabbit; one single, short, staccato bark. That bark was another woodland warning signal which was heeded instantly by the tiniest, most beautiful spotted kid, which leapt up from just beyond the bank, and chased into the bushes after the doe. It's the only time I have ever heard the bark of the roe deer, but I couldn't have asked for a better example of its purpose and effectiveness.

On reflection, my one mistake was in not looking more closely at the ground beyond that sheltered bank. Roe deer frequently give birth to twins, and it's quite possible that another tiny kid may have ignored the warning and stayed put in the shadows.

There was one occasion when I like to think I saved a roe deer from disaster. As I was driving through the Blackdown Hills in Somerset, a roe-deer doe dashed across the road in front of my car. Roe have tremendous agility, and this one was no sluggard. Having crossed the road, the prospect before it was daunting. A steep bank rose some twenty feet from the roadside, topped by a stretch of chestnut paling.

The doe scrambled the bank in a flurry of moss and earth, and, confronted with the paling, tried to clear it. She took off from the bank with all the panache of a well trained show-jumper facing a puissance fence, but it was an impossible task. She just hadn't the

impetus or the room at the summit, and all she succeeded in doing, was getting stuck between two pales.

There she was, stuck fast, with no chance of escape. The pales gripped her at the thinnest part of the body, just in front of her hind quarters and her front legs were unable to touch the ground on the other side of the fence. This deer was well and truly trapped, and would more than likely fall prey to some marauding dog, come darkness, as the strength left her body in the unequal struggle.

It's not a job I would recommend, but I had to release that deer. The only way was to grab the two hind feet and try to lift them clear of the fence. The two problems were the weight of the deer and the hooves, sharp as cut-throat razors. The moment I tried to grab them I was rewarded by aggressive kicks. Having sorted out the problem so that I stood on one side of the deer, and holding the feet so that I couldn't be slashed by those horny hooves, I managed to lift her clear. She was gone in a flash. As I say, it wasn't an easy job, but it seemed to me only fair that a creature so well equipped for survival should be given a little help by the species that had placed her in this unfair situation.

Mi Casa, Su Casa

I did consider letting the Electoral Registration Officer know about it, but I thought it might lead to endless and pointless communications, although it did seem, on the face of it, that Esmeralda came within the orbit of his enquiries. She's a resident, she's under our roof, but the snag is that she's produced young, and for the life of me, I not only don't know how many offspring there are, but I don't even know to which parts of the house they've dispersed.

She lives, I should explain, in the loo. She's been there for weeks stuck in one corner, as if waiting for the other old lady, and looking down on all she surveys with the air of a queen. She is, I should also explain, a spider, and, although we like to think the small room is not only neat and tidy but hygienic as well, she obviously finds a living in there somehow.

When we put a roof over our heads, we are making not just a home for ourselves, but a habitat with all mod cons for a whole range of other living creatures, from things we can't even see with the naked eye, to a selection of creepy-crawlies and even small mammals. For most of these creatures, a crack under a door, a hole in a wall, a gap between roof tiles, is like writing a large 'welcome' all over the front door mat.

Spiders always seem to be the first colonisers. The moment the builders have gone out of the front door, there they are. In fact, I rather think they move in with the builders, and, for some people, finding a large, long-legged house spider in the bath knocks a couple of hundred pounds off the value there and then. It's fairly clear, though, why spiders move in so soon. While the house is being built, with the walls up, and holes where the windows and doors will be eventually, there's a glorious opportunity for spiders to spin a web.

Partly built houses provide lovely nooks and crannies with a breeze blowing through them, that are bound to channel all sorts of flying insects along the flight path. The spiders take advantage of the situation and, with a warm and cosy space above, under the tiles, what better conditions could be asked for. There it is, shelter, warmth and ideal trapping conditions all provided. It's little wonder that any of us moving into new houses find that we already have lodgers. Nor do they confine themselves to surburban semis, but will make their way into the upper storeys of modern high rise blocks long before the last of the builders' rubble has left the site.

I'm not one for putting a large boot in where spiders are concerned. The smaller ones can stay as long as they like, because they do help to clear the place of house flies, if there should be any around. However, when I see one of the larger ones, sidling across the carpet like a crab, pretending it isn't even there, then I draw the line. Even so the boot is not the answer, nor, indeed, is it when we find 'old hairy' in the bath. I reckon that although they look nasty and frighten many people, the thing to do is to shove them outside the back door. They are quite harmless and so my patent remedy for disposing of them will not result in a confrontation. No spider in the British Isles bites, unless Uncle George has returned from a package tour in foreign parts with a black widow.

To dispose of the big fellows, stalk your spider with a wine glass. Creep up on it and slap the glass over the beast, (a glass is better than a cup, in that you can see whether you've trapped it or missed it). Then slip a stiffish piece of paper or a postcard under the glass

and quickly turn the glass over. Now it can't get out because the sides of the glass are too slippery. Quick march to the door and empty your spider out into the elements. Mind you, it will probably be back again, crabbing along the skirting board within a couple of nights, but it makes an interesting battle. From my experience, we usually win.

I have one further word on the species. Those found in the bath don't come up the waste pipe. They might have come in through the overflow pipe, although, more probably, they fell into the bath from the ceiling. But they never come up the waste pipe because that has a U bend in it, constantly filled with water.

Old houses, naturally, have a much higher population of wild life than new, but bats, these days, are being pushed out altogether. They are being denied habitat by the renovation of old cottages and churches, where the parochial councils can afford such luxuries. Even potholers are not entirely blameless. Off they go, determined young men and women in search of adventure, into holes and caverns, often putting their own lives and the lives of people who have to be called out to rescue them in danger. That's their affair, but I do wish they wouldn't go into caves where bats hibernate for the winter.

I've been in such holes—not very far, since I suffer desperately from claustrophobia—but in the places I've been during the winter months, I've seen bats revived from hibernation by the slight rise in temperature caused by the heat radiated from our own bodies. Even by breathing on them, you can see the slow return of the bat from its state of hibernation to the point where it starts to flex the beautiful wing membranes that give it flight. Unfortunately, if a bat should re-awake and there is no insect life around, it's chances of survival are slim.

Those rectors with bats in their belfries and death watch beetle in their roof timbers, might do well to consider the profit and loss account. The bats' droppings in the pews may cause annoyance to the worthy worshippers, whose support is vital for the church restoration fund, but as long as the bats are allowed to stay in the tower, steeple or roof, they will keep down the population of death watch beetles.

Not all roof-dwellers are so co-operative. If you've ever slept in an old house, just under the roof space, you may have heard the sound of marching feet above your head during the night hours. The imagination can run riot. The feet sound like an army in full pursuit of the enemy. In the house I'm thinking of, the culprits were certainly starlings, but in some places there's no doubt that mice and rats could be to blame.

Some birds are welcome to share the roof of our house, others are kept at bay. This discrimination provokes the inevitable question; am I a lover of all birds, or just some of them? Putting myself in the latter category, I won't have house sparrows in the roof. House sparrows take advantage of us to such a degree that they outstay their welcome. If you put food out on a bird table no matter how much craft and guile you use in placing food where only the birds you particularly want to see can get at it, the cheeky sparrows will be the first on the scene to take the pickings, long before the shy species get a look in.

The same strictures apply to their nesting habits. A pair had a nest under our roof last year and they've done a quick recce of the site this year. But I'm not having that, and the tiny hole they've found will have to be blocked up. Even so I reckon they'll find another spot because they weren't the only residents.

Last year, we also had house martins with us. They were marvellous birds who stayed and twittered right the way through, into the autumn, until they left their muddy nest under the roof and fled southwards on their winter migration flight. They made a mess with their droppings, but we were prepared to put up with this because they are such good companions. As long as they are still around, you feel that summer can't be over.

This particular family was waiting for its delinquent member to get ready. Day after day, the parent birds would return with food for this one loner, who'd take occasional forays from the nest onto the wall and promptly hop back in again. Eventually he left with the rest, but his chances of making the long journey to South Africa we reckoned to be slight. Having watched their departure, we don't subscribe to the theory that martins hibernate!

That house martins' nest will undoubtedly be the sparrows' next port of call once we've denied them the roof, but that port, too, I shall close by pulling down the old martins' nest. It wouldn't be much good to them for another year anyway. They'll build again in the same place and, by removing the old structure, I'm not only denying the house sparrows a ready made nest, I'm helping the house martins as well.

The list of lodgers is endless, and only the annual spring-clean will really show us what shelter our little semi has provided. There will be ladybirds behind the curtains, and there'll be the odd but-terfly here and there which has holed up for the winter, probably a tortoiseshell or a peacock. There are certainly moths, and, if they've left any thread in the carpet, there will be carpet beetles as well. Wood lice, those strange mini-armadillo looking things, seem to find their way in as well, and even aphids on the beautiful potted plant which came as a welcome Christmas present.

Sometimes in taking over a property, we take over the lodgers as well. An acquaintance inherited a colony of bees along with his elegant manor house. There were there when he came in, and there they stay, despite the occasional stings that his spaniels have to suffer from the avalanche of dying drones annually thrown out from the colony. Although bees in the eaves may not appeal to everyone, it's as well to think hard before treating all uninvited guests as unwelcome ones as well.

But Don't Call It Fred

A dying duckling in a thunderstorm is a pitiful sight, as is any small bird only just out of the nest and not capable of fending for itself. Often it is the first shower of rain that the small bird has experienced, and its plaintive cheeping is enough to bring tears to the eyes of many a well meaning naturalist. Sometimes the kids come home with a tiny thrush stuck in the typical schoolboy pocket, a bird stuck up with toffee papers, grubby, grimy, patently on its last legs.

Every spring I'm asked advice on what to do with an abandoned bird, and suppressing any non-ornithological thoughts, I try to point out as gently as possible that the bird, the fledgling, should not have been picked up and brought home it should have been left alone. The noises it made indicated very strongly that it was lost, that it had fallen from the nest and become separated from the parent bird, but the plaintive calls were really a case of the bird trying to make contact again with the parent, and not with us. It's pretty certain that the female parent would not have been far away, but because of our presence when the chick was found, was staying very much out of sight. This is only natural, and more often than not, once we've moved out of the territory, the parent bird would sort out the whole thing for itself, and gather up its wayward offspring.

It is possible that we could have very good cause for thinking that the lonely chick is without a parent, because, say, we've seen its mutilated body, not a few yards away from the cheeping chick. Do not forget, however, that the chick has two parents, and should one have died, the feeding operation will usually be carried on successfully, if somewhat frantically, by the survivor.

Not so long ago I came across the nesting tree of a tawny owl, a fine site in a hole in an old oak tree. From all the signs the nest was very much in use; the droppings splashed over the vegetation around the tree were extremely fresh and so too, were the pellets. Far from fresh was the carcase, sadly, of one adult tawny owl lying among the leaves between two root forks of the tree.

The carcase was too decomposed to send away for analysis, but, from its position under the nest site, I can only assume that it had eaten poisoned flesh and, after returning to the tree, had then succumbed. That sad fact apart, the remaining bird was still busy at the nest and, as this was the time of the year when owlets would almost be at the flying stage, the surviving parent bird, even though it had lost its mate, was still concentrating on bringing up the young.

On another occasion, driving through an Oxfordshire lane in the dusk, I came across the tiny strutting form of a young lapwing, looking like a ball of fluff on stilts. Just over the hedge, an adult lapwing was making agitated calls trying to get the young one back again. This was once again a case for leaving well alone.

There are of course, exceptions to the rule. I remember the story of a family in Dorset who had found a tiny swallow that had fallen from the nest. The nest was inaccessible and the nestling certainly had no chance of flying back itself. So these good people took the young swallow under their wing, lavishing on it every kindness, feeding it chopped-up bits of meat with a pair of tweezers and drops of fluid from a fountain pen sac.

The treatment went on for weeks but they were not concerned with making a pet of the bird, knowing full well that come the autumn, some inner urge in that tiny swallow would make it head away south on migration. In their house, they had a conservatory, and if there's one thing a conservatory will do besides provide warmth for exotic plants, it will act as a fly trap. So instead of getting out the insect spray, the flies in the conservatory were allowed to flit about.

The next step was to teach the young swallow, now able to get airborne for a few short yards, that flies in the conservatory window would be much better food than bits of chopped meat. The swallow eventually got the idea of fending for itself, and cleared up the flies in the conservatory. From that, it was but a short step to giving the bird its freedom and, thanks to the commonsense attitude of its human foster parents, that bird had at least a chance of survival in the wild, where it belonged.

This underlines the one great danger of taking any wild creature into our homes. They become so reliant on us for food that we replace the real parents and, if kept in captivity for long enough, they reach the stage of never again recognising their own kind. Scientists call this 'imprinting' and it need not be a human association which brings this about. It could be the cardboard box in which the bird or animal was first kept. The box has replaced the parent image. And once this imprinting has taken place, the chances of the creature surviving again in the wild are very remote.

Other dangers are more clearly visible. Take the bird that has flown full tilt into the french windows and has knocked itself out. Here is a case for picking it up, sticking it in a box for a while until it revives, as it usually will. The important thing is to release the bird again as soon as possible. If it has a broken leg or wing, then consult an expert. It's worth remembering however that in the case of severely oiled sea birds, even though they may be cleaned up and released again, not many of them live for very long after. These days official policy turns more and more to putting an oiled or injured bird out of its misery as quickly as possible.

Misery among our own young often results from apparently heartless action, but this is the moment for a basic lesson. Its vitally important, I think, to educate our children to consider wild birds and wild animals as being quite apart from ourselves. This is the moment to outline the dangers of anthropomorphism. Birds and animals do not possess human attributes and should not be given names. The young of any creature in the wild is not a baby, it is only humans who have babies. Use the right words, chicks, cubs, calves, fawns, and never encourage the thought that fledgling thrushes have a mum and dad. They are parent birds. They can't talk either, communicate yes, but never the conversation in words. Even our pets, our dogs and cats, despite what some proud owners may think, do not understand the words we say to them. They do react to the tone of our voices. Try 'there's a good dog', in the tone normally reserved for chastising it, and see what happens.

Apart from the fact that it is illegal to capture and cage our native birds and certainly illegal to keep many animals as pets, there are other dangers. I well remember the case of a young grey squirrel that had become partly tame and then had either escaped or had been given its freedom. It had certainly been handled, and once in the wild again was very soon on the scrounge for food. It came to the window sill to collect hazel nuts that were placed out every morning for the benefit of the local nuthatches.

All that came to a sudden stop, however, when one day, my daughter was taking out the morning supply of nuts. The squirrel came scurrying along, climbed right up her body to her shoulder, producing some very nasty scratches on the way. The result was one very frightened child. Whether that squirrel ever survived I neither know nor care, but it had certainly lost its fear of humans.

The same thing happens with fox cubs kept as pets. When that call of the wild lures them back to the countryside, they become veritable killers. They come closer than ever to our houses, nearer than ever to chicken runs, and to poultry wandering over a field of stubble, and, unlike the truly wild fox, this half tame animal becomes a daylight prowler.

This is the fox, which, because of its lack of fear, the countryman dreads. It's the fox that someone had on a lead and doted on like a pet dog—and probably called Fred.

Detergents and Deterrents

'It's the industrialists who are to blame for all this pollution, look at that ghastly black oil flowing out of that factory waste pipe straight into the river.' Thus runs the reaction of any con-servationist on seeing a blatant infraction of our conservation laws. In my experience, these abuses are most obvious from carriage windows as the train speeds through the outskirts of an industrial town. The back of the factory, never seen by those who pass the elegant portals of its front entrance, tells its ugly story only to the weary traveller. Such places don't often advertise their names, so it's difficult to place the blame at the right front door, and even if you do write a 'disgusted of Tunbridge Wells' type letter to the newspapers, it doesn't really do much good.

The same irate traveller gets equally hot under the collar when he sees a river or stream covered with thick detergent foam; his face becomes as purple as the river is white with his condemnation of industry and dark satanic mills. But is he not to blame as well, our traveller? Aren't we all to blame? Aren't we all individually multiplying the pollution problem in our own little way?

Take the man who services his own car on a Saturday morning to cut down on his motoring costs. All very necessary these days with garage charges being what they are, you may say, but, whereas garages are properly equipped to handle every aspect of servicing, the DIY man often is not. When it comes to changing the engine oil in his faithful old jalopy, he is faced with a problem. Where should he put the old and mucky oil that drains out of the sump, like nearly solidified black treacle. It just so happens there is a roadside drain right outside his black door, and so he carefully deposits the old oil straight down the drain. He's got rid of it, he doesn't have any use at all for it, it's gone, out of sight, out of mind. But he is every bit as guilty of polluting the environment as the factory manager who allows waste products to flow into a convenient stream.

After our economy-minded DIY man has finished his filthy work, off he goes indoors to tell his ever-loving the good news, that the old bus is good for thousands more miles yet, and with the money he's saved they can have a darned good holiday after all. She takes one look at the state of his clothes and orders him straight to the bathroom. 'And bring those filthy trousers and shirt down with you when you come, I'll put them in the washing machine right away.'

House proud is the ever-loving and into the machine go the garments. 'Now how much detergent should I use?' she asks herself, 'The instructions on the packet say a cup full, let's put in two to make sure I get Bert's filthy trousers clean.' That's just what she does, and blithely watches the foam flowing away down the sink afterwards, again out of sight, out of mind. Another polluter has joined the ranks of the guilty.

Our car-servicing friend has a next door neighbour who is also anxious to keep down his garage bills. He, too, does the work himself, but he is a bit brighter. He wouldn't dream of letting his old engine oil soak away through the council drains because he's a fisherman, and he knows that the oil might find its way into his favourite stream and kill all his fish. So very carefully he drains off his engine into an old tin bath and then with an old funnel he pours the oil into a five gallon drum, which he uses every time he services the car. When it's full he can get rid of it.

He's the man who has become known to countrymen as the streaker in clothes, because you might see him stop his car in a quiet lane and suddenly become a furtive fugitive. He'll get out of the car almost on tip-toe, look this way and that to make sure no one is about, and then dash to the boot of the car, fling it open, grab his five gallon drum of old oil, shut the boot, and taking one quick glance around, throw the drum over the hedge. Before it's landed on the other side, he's back in the driving seat. There's probably a par time for such feats, and our man deserves a place in *The Guiness Book of Records*. He's the all time champion when it comes to getting rid of old oil. He's got a town full of mates. They're the ones who dump anything they don't need just about anywhere; from a rusted out car that won't pass the MOT test, to the pram that helped raise all the kids. I've seen the lot in my travels, bikes with and without engines, 'fridges, cookers, metal bedsteads, mattresses that even the moths have deserted; the waste products of the effluent society.

The blame can't be laid only at the door of the thoughtless individual, it must also be handed on like the hot chestnut it is to that great anonymous body, 'Authority.' Many council refuse-collection services just will not take away large items of rubbish on their weekly collection. Oh yes, they are quite prepared to make a special journey to take it away, but, 'we do make a charge guv.'

It's small wonder that more and more of us are driven to indiscriminate dumping: in fields, woods, lanes and ponds, dumping that is dangerous to life in the countryside. Children and livestock are injured by jagged metal or broken bottles. Ponds and streams are poisoned. Large parts of the countryside become weeping sores on the landscape of what we fondly call our 'green and pleasant land.'

95

Part of that pleasant land, Mr. Semi-detached Suburban likes to have around his castle in the form of a neat and well tended garden, full of prize roses and with a pocket handkerchief lawn that would do the local bowling club proud. In his cheek by jowl existence with his next door neighbours however, he can't burn up his garden rubbish, and he probably lives in a smokeless zone. He's tried hiding his rose prunings in bundles in his rubbish bin, and his lawn trimmings, but the refuse collectors spotted that little ploy, and made it quite clear that it's only household refuse they deal with, not anything from the garden.

Our subject is, by nature, a tidy man—his garden is evidence of that—and so he buys half a dozen of those green plastic bags designed just for his needs, for his garden garbage. Into the bag it goes, and, when it's full, he too joins the evening dash to the countryside. The problem posed by this type is not insurmountable. Some local authorities have taken the right approach in having official tips where we can take our rubbish. It may be an old disused quarry, which, once filled, can be grassed over again. We shall have helped to get rid of what used to be a scar, and also to restore a small piece of the land that is so precious.

Of course, the time is fast approaching in this greedy consumer world when all our waste will have to be recycled. Human sewage, for instance, will be composted—as it already is in the Channel island of Jersey—to feed back to the land and increase our crops. Indestructible plastic containers will be collected separately and made into usable plastics again. Tin cans will go back to the steel industry, waste paper back to the paper mills, and all bottles will be returnable. All this will take place not only because we are making a convenience of the countryside, but also because we shall need to preserve for re-use the very stuff which we now regard as 'disposable' rubbish.

Radio Nature Trails

There are a few moments in everyone's lifetime, which are treasured above all others. These special moments, when a door into another world is briefly and suddenly opened, permitting just a glimpse inside, are, for most people, a once-in-a-lifetime experience.

Over the past few years, however, I have been unusually lucky. My work has taken me to places that have revealed quite a few of these special moments. During the making of the radio series, 'The Living World', I have happened on some unforgettable sounds and sights—and not a few hazards; but, of all the programmes in that series, the ones that have brought me closest to the countryside have been the 'Radio Nature Trail' broadcasts.

Who could forget, for instance, a cold winter's day, with the hoar-frosted fens glistening white in the sunshine like an enormous Christmas cake? On that morning, the weak winter sun melted the ice on the water with a sound like distant gunfire, and we could hear the plaintive honking of Bewick's swans, and the whistling chorus of wigeon and teal in the background.

It was these sounds, coming over clearly in accompaniment of our commentary, that, I hope, brought the whole area alive to the audience at home, and made them, to some extent, viewers as well, enjoying with us that awesomely beautiful morning out on the bleak fenlands.

It was on the success of this curious alchemy, which could make the ears see, that the 'Radio Nature Trails' depended, on our ability to convey something of what we saw, with the help of background sounds, to our listeners. The opportunities to add this extra dimension to our information on what was to be seen were varied, and often unexpected; a robin's autumn song, mute swans interrupting conversation with the pulsing, reedy *obbligato* of their wings, even the snuffling of rats on a Thameside rubbish tip gave the audience a chance to do a little more than simply listen.

For me, the first of these broadcasting adventures began on a blustery February morning in the middle of Plymouth Sound, as Tony Soper, the distinguished west-country naturalist, and I prepared to take a trip up the Tamar with our listeners. When Dilys Breese, producer of the 'Living World' programmes, and myself met up with Tony Soper that morning, we had little idea of what we were in for, nor of the problems that would be posed by a half-hour programme, recorded on board a launch with a portable tape-recorder.

It wasn't, on the face of it, the ideal day for such an adventure, because the seas were coming into the sound with some force. Tony and I chatted about razorbills, gannets and gulls, to the raucous accompaniment of wind and waves, and did our best to stay dry. All this came over in the recording, and our listeners were left in no doubt that it was rough in Plymouth Sound.

We didn't stay long in the vicinity of the breakwater! I'm the sort of sailor who gets sea-sick watching a rolling ship on the television screen, and, thankfully, as we turned back towards the Naval Dockyard, past the laid-up ships, the waters became smoother and the wind subsided. It was even better in the estuary of the Tamar itself, and whenever we saw or heard something interesting, Dilys switched on the tape machine and Tony and I chatted or listened with our audience to the sounds.

With the added bonus of the calls of many of the birds, the lapping of the waves against the side of the boat, and even the sounds of the boat engine starting and stopping, it was possible to paint a sound picture almost as vivid as a colour TV film of the same situation. Thanks to Tony's expert knowledge of the Tamar River and its wildlife, and his ability to talk about the various species with such enthusiasm, our nature ramble seemed to work.

For me, one of the highlights was seeing at close quarters the flock of long-legged waders with upturned bills that spent the winter on the estuary, the avocets.

So we left Plymouth, and Dilys then had the task of editing all the recordings into a programme. It went on the air on Sunday, 8 March 1970 and, since then, there has been a Radio Nature Trail every single month. In that time we've ranged far and wide in the British Isles, and occasionally even abroad. For me, they've been exciting years, and, if there's one thing I've come to expect of the Nature Trails, it is that the unexpected is often round the corner.

An instance of this occurred when we went to Wheatfen Broad to see my old friend, the distinguished Norfolk naturalist, Ted Ellis. Ted is the most engaging chap, and enthusiastic about his corner of the Broads and their acres of reed beds. He knows his way through them in the height of summer when they grow to eyebrow level just as surely as he does in the winter when the reeds have been harvested and his so-called footpaths are almost visible. There we were, struggling through what to me felt like elephant grass. Ted puffed at his pipe, and I smoked cigarette after cigarette in a vain attempt to keep some of the mosquitoes at bay. It was not exactly easy going, particularly as I had binoculars round my neck, a recording machine over one shoulder and a shooting stick in the hand not holding the cigarette.

Ted warned us, that somewhere soon we should come across a

'ligger', a plank of wood spanning a dyke. We found it all right. I suppose fen folk are used to such precarious bridges over deep and dirty waters. The snag was that, in the lush undergrowth of reed, it wasn't possible to see either the edge of the ditch or the beginning of the narrow plank. I missed the latter and found the former, falling right into the filthy stinking water, fortunately without damaging either the recording machine or the binoculars.

Ted was not content with that escapade, and there was more to come. We had a mysterious meeting planned with a boat, but it hadn't been explained how crucial the appointment was until we found the waters of the broad rising, and Ted insisting that we hurry. More wet feet, even damper clothes were our lot, and, when we reached the boat, it looked about as sea-worthy as the plank across the ditch. However, it floated and got us back safely, wet, weary and bitten from head to toe. The red weals of mosquito bites stayed with me for a fortnight after. It was fun, but, since that day, I've never set out on any Radio Nature Trail without a complete change of clothing.

The wisdom of that decision was brought home to all of us on a trip that same year to Scotland. Loch Lomond was the place, and its banks that day were anything but bonny. We met up with Eddie Idle of the Nature Conservancy early in the morning to take yet another boat trip to Inchcailloch, one of the five islands that form the National Nature Reserve on the Loch. As we met, the rain started falling, but there was no postponing the event. Dilys and I had to catch an evening flight from Glasgow Airport, and so, with Eddie's warning that there is no wetter place on earth when it's pouring with rain than a boat in the middle of Loch Lomond, we set off for Inchcailloch.

We were soaked to the skin long before we landed on the island. The rain came down all the time we were there, and didn't stop until we rejoined the boat later in the afternoon. People afterwards remarked that the rain added atmosphere; for my part it did give me an opportunity to test again the efficacy of Scotland's native remedy for ills and chills!

Recording programmes on wet, overcast days though, has its advantages. The weather cuts down the flying capabilities of both military and commercial aircraft. If there's one thing we've come to hate, it's low flying aircraft. Just as you're in the middle of talking about a badger set or trying to catch the elusive song of a lark high above your head, it's almost inevitable that there'll be a dull whine in the distance, getting louder and louder as a turbo-propped aircraft drowns everything in the passage overhead. Worse still is the sudden 'whoosh' of a military aircraft going so fast that its ear-shattering roar follows after the 'plane has gone by.

On one occasion, Pat Morris took us on a tour of what he described as 'one of the largest, unspoilt open spaces near London,

Esher Common.' We started on the trail just seventeen miles from St. Paul's Cathedral, close to the main London to Portsmouth road, and, above the noise of the traffic, we could hear the twittering of blue tits in the trees over our heads. However, that was not all that we heard. It was very soon painfully obvious that we were bang underneath one of the flight paths into Heathrow.

Even worse than Esher Common though, was the frustrating day, not to mention part of the night as well, that we spent on the Wash, not far from Kings Lynn. The fact that we would have to cross a causeway at low tide to reach an artificial island and then stay there until the island disappeared or the tide receded, didn't cause us undue worry. After all, we were in good hands with the Director of the British Trust for Ornithology, Jim Flegg, and his amply proportioned colleague, Chris Mead. If all else failed he would float us off!

We reached the island at dawn and, shortly after we arrived, so did the aircraft. Fast military aircraft like Phantoms and Lightnings came flashing past on manoeuvres. What we hadn't bargained for either was the bombing range, a few miles away. Those infernal machines came in at thirty second intervals for the best part of three hours, and we were eventually reduced to recording the programme in ten second bursts, timing it so that we started talking as the jets disappeared towards the horizon.

We've come to realise from bitter experience over the years, that there are very few places in these islands of ours where it's possible to enjoy complete quiet. Noise is as much a pollutant and a blight on our lives as toxic chemicals. Ironically, we have been asked, and often by people who should know better, whether the sounds on our programmes were put in afterwards?' We get a bit touchy about remarks like that. The only sounds we broadcast are the ones we hear ourselves, and record as we go along the trails.

It is possible, though, to get away from aircraft underground. I pass on that information secondhand for the very good reason that caves and I don't get on. If a cave is of the 'stand up and walk in' variety, I can just about bear it, but if it means crawling through a tiny grating into the inky blackness on your belly, then I'm afraid I have to chicken out. I've tried, believe me I've tried, but claustrophobia takes over and I just can't go on. So, on a couple of Nature Trails, I've stayed out in the air, while the producer and more intrepid souls braved the deeps of caves.

Heights too are not my happiest companions, but I've managed to come to terms with them far more than with caves, and I think that I can thank my friends of the Royal Society for the Protection of Birds for helping me to clear that particular barrier. Anthony Clay, the Society's Film Officer, was making a documentary about herons, and, so that he could get some good close-up shots of the herons and their young in the nests, he'd organised a hide in the tree tops, right on the edge of a heronry. The hide was just under a hundred feet high, and approached by ladders connecting a series of scaffolded platforms.

We spent the best part of a day up in the hide which could accommodate five of us, at a pinch. We did knock off for lunch during the period of the day when there seemed to be least activity in the heronry, and that meant climbing down to ground level again, and returning up the shaky ladders a couple of hours later. Apart from aching limbs, there were no ill effects, and, after that experience, I was almost agile when it came to climbing a fire watchers' tower in the Forest of Dean.

There have actually been some injuries on Radio Nature Trails, and one of them might have been serious. Indeed we might have been left without a programme for one particular week, had Dr. Ernest Neal been rushed off to hospital. We were just landing on the island of Steepholm in the Bristol Channel, and Ernest, being our guide for the day, stepped ashore first onto the rocks. Now, Steepholm is heavily populated with gulls and their droppings are everywhere. As he went out of the boat with the agility of a ten year old, Ernest slipped and gave himself a rather nasty knock. We made sympathetic noises and, making sure he wasn't wobbling with concussion, went about recording another Nature Trail.

In fact there could easily have been other injuries that day, since we were right bang in the middle of the gulls' breeding season. The nests were so thick that it was almost impossible not to step on eggs or wayward chicks, but the real danger lay in the adult gulls who showed a marked dislike of intruders and kept buzzing us. This is all very well when you can see the bird coming towards you. We soon found that we could spot a possible 'buzzer' by its flight behaviour, but what we hadn't bargained for were the extraordinarily crafty blighters who buzzed from behind. The first we knew of that was a 'whoosh' by our ears like a jet aircraft. Fortunately no blood was spilt.

One day blood was shed in the interests of the programme. We had been recording in the Forest of Dean with Bruce Campbell, and we had along with us a young student who is a super-keen ornithologist. He knew of a tawny owl which he'd had under observation for some weeks. There were now owlets in the nest and Bruce was anxious to ring them. There we were at the base of this tree, the nest hole not more than ten feet high, and Nigel was up there. He handed down the young birds, Bruce carefully ringed them, and we handed them back up the tree to our climbing colleague. At that moment he came down to the ground with a wallop, holding his forehead which was streaming with blood. Our first reaction was that he had slipped, until in that split second we saw an adult tawny owl flying away. We knew that the parent bird was around from the agitation among the blackbirds nearby, but she had flown to her nest without the slightest sound, and then buzzed our friend. She had not only buzzed him, but had given him a nasty scratch on the head with her sharp talons. We were naturally concerned that he, at least, get medical treatment for the wound, but he would not hear of it. Indeed, I think he regarded it as an honourable battle scar.

As I've said, Radio Nature Trails often come up with the unexpected, and they have taught me a great deal about this country of ours. My eyes have been opened as never before, as I've chatted to the experts, and been guided along their favourite paths. Despite their tutoring, I still can't sort out all the similar songs of some of our warblers, small lichens will always be a mystery to me; and, as for edible fungi, I shall stick firmly to the only ones I'm really sure about, the good old field mushrooms. But, from each and every one of the guides on Radio Nature Trails, I have learned something new. I thank them all, but above all I would like to pay tribute to our producer, Dilys Breese, who has had to bear the brunt of the work involved in making the programmes presentable. The hours she has had to spend editing out our fluffs and making everything fit together, are never shown in terms of paid overtime, only in a love for the programme itself, and, something all of us who go Radio Nature Trailing share, a concern for the countryside.

Graveyard or Larder

The motoring map of this country is a web of fast motorways drawing opposite ends of this country ever closer together. Not everyone's joy is unconfined at this, and some people have already discerned a large spider sitting in the centre of the web. Conservationists spotted the monster from afar, they saw the roads as death traps, not to drivers hell-bent on their own destruction, but to our flora and fauna.

Their arguments were highly persuasive. Consider the larger mammals; deer, badgers and foxes. They are very much creatures of habit, invariably going from place to place in the countryside, following well defined tracks. Cut those tracks, those arteries, with a motorway, and the animals are going to die. They would stick to their tracks and be killed by fast moving traffic.

There was the equally plausible argument put forward, that the territories of certain species would be decimated. The countryside would become a series of smaller living spaces and, because a given area can only support a given number of any one species, the surplus would try to move out and also be killed in the process. It wasn't only the large mammals that caused the furore. The smaller ones too, it was argued, would suffer; the hedgehogs, rabbits and hares. Even the birds would not go unscathed; in flying across the motorway, they too would fall foul of the motorist.

Undoubtedly some of these fears were well-founded, but I can't help wondering if, in the final count, things have turned out as black as the conservationists painted them when they first uttered their dark warnings.

What we tend to forget is that a motorway is no instant happening. It isn't something which sprouts into being like a mushroom overnight, as anyone who has had to live by a new section of road knows only too well. Living near a mammoth engineering enterprise such as that can be a round the clock nightmare. Dark is turned into day by arc lamps, the noise of the machinery is deafening, and sleep becomes impossible.

If that's the effect it has on us, what then of the wildlife of the countryside? They are far more susceptible to disturbance than we are, and that disturbance makes itself felt on the very day that the first tons of earth or rock are carved out from what was field or woodland, hill or plain. It's right there and then that the mammals will be seeking fresh territories, making new tracks, and not when the motor vehicles are speeding along in their seventies.

In many thousand miles of motorway driving, I have never seen a dead badger on the hard shoulder or central reservation. I have seen only one dead fox, and not a single deer. The slaughter of these animals, particularly the badgers, takes place on the other roads of the country, roads with grassy banks and green hedges on either side, places where the animals can find natural cover before making their dash across the roadway. In this argument too, I think we can include our song birds. They frequent woodland and hedgerows, not wide motorways, bounded by only wire fences. Their numbers are not decimated by the seventy miles an hour speed fiend, but by the fifty miles an hour man on the lesser roads.

I know only too well that it is widely believed that there is a tremendous toll of wild life along the motorway. The proof is often given that there must be plenty of carrion lying around, those birds and animals killed by cars, because of the number of crows seen scratching about on the verges. Those crows are there, it is said, because there are plenty of easy pickings, because they are clearing up the carcasses. I can only refer people to the old country saying about crows. It is observed that if you see a lot of crows together they are rooks, and if a rook is seen alone, it is a crow.

Undoubtedly some crows are finding carrion, but this is mainly small mammals, the voles and mice, that try to scamper across the expanses of tarmac and either die of heart failure or get hit by the traffic in the attempt.

Just a few of the casualties may be bigger mammals, but, from my own observations, I can only say that, of the birds that frequent the motorways, the majority are particularly agile at getting out of the way. Even those rooks, the few crows and sometimes jackdaws which I see, seem to have come to terms with the speed of the traffic, and time their movement to a nicety. Very few of them end up as tangled masses of feather and bone, and those that do are invariably inexperienced young.

Further evidence that the smaller mammals colonize near these roads is backed up by the unquestionable success of one member of the hawk family, the kestrel. It's almost become a motorway pastime to amuse the children by spying kestrels, those beautiful birds of prey, hovering in the eye of the wind. Kestrels have cottoned on to the good living that the grassy banks provide. There they are, acre upon acre, ideal habitat for animals like voles. Good living for voles means, in turn, good feeding for kestrels,—live voles, not carcasses—and the better the food supply, the greater number of young kestrels that not only fledge, but fly. It's a fairly simple equation. Kestrels have increased in number throughout the country because of the coming of those motorways, and those beautiful birds of prey certainly haven't fallen foul of the motor car.

If the Ministry of Transport should decide that every acre of grass should become just another space to plant a tree, I think that would be more than a pity, it would be a crime. Destroy that grassland habitat, and we should destroy the very conditions that have indirectly helped the kestrel population. We should destroy at the same time the stretches that are just beginning to blossom in another way, with wild flowers. Bunches of cowslips and oxslips are springing up. Banks of poppies and even wild daffodils are now to be seen.

Those grassy banks, are genuine nature reserves with the added advantage that we, the motorists, can't stop and trample all over them, that is, unless we have the unhappy experience of a breakdown. It's an ill wind. . . .

Harvest in the Sky

The first indication that something unusual was happening came when lounging on the garden deck-chairs suddenly became impossible. It wasn't that the sun was too hot, it was a perfect tanning August afternoon. The trouble was the irritation to the skin from insects that settled everywhere. First of all, they came in ones and twos, that could be brushed away with a flick of the hand. Then they came in legions and drove the sunbathers in doors. From behind the protection of french windows, it was possible to see the next stage of this strange phenomenon that comes round once a year like a slightly movable feast day.

A feast day indeed it is, for the birds. The house martins were the first to spot the chance of the feast around our garden. There was the striking spectacle of martins actually fluttering to the ground, or resting, uncharacteristically, on the edge of the pavements and pecking around in great excitement. Clearly, they weren't collecting mud for nest building this late in the year. Their antics then became more conventional as they left the ground and flew around the houses, skimming the roads and rooftops and gradually working higher and higher into the air.

Then above the martins, the sky became filled with gulls galore, wheeling in fantastic aerobatics; diving steeply and pulling out by impossible body contortions, switching direction to steep climbs until they reached stalling speed, and then falling away to gain more air speed. The activity of these herring gulls, black-headed gulls and black-backed gulls spelled extraordinary excitement, as if they had been afflicted by an avian equivalent of St. Vitus's dance. Nor were they alone.

Up on their open ballet stage, even a rook could be seen like a black robber taking advantage of the feast. Higher still, through binoculars it was possible to pick out those most beautiful and aerobatic birds, the swifts, scything through the sky. One bird, not normally given to taking food on the wing, was also attracted by the activity. A common house sparrow, doing a very poor imitation of a spotted flycatcher, went through the motions of chasing one of the insects.

This was the day of the flying ants. I suppose I should have expected it, for, over a lunch-time drink in the local some two hours earlier, one topic of conversation had been the ants. People said that they were crawling everywhere, and all the usual pieces of advice and age-old remedies were being freely given. Kettles of boiling water seemed to be the popular choice, but some had bought up ant repellant powders from the village store. Dark mutterings from those who knew the dangers of DDT powder were met with some surprise. Surely the problem was to get rid of those ants.

Of course, they were talking about crawling ants, the workers from the colonies, and presumably all this activity reported from the village gardens was the overture to the afternoon's dance in the sky. Those martins, perched at the pavement's edge, had been the first to spot the emergence from cracks and crevices of the males and queens, the winged members of the colony. On this one suitably hot day every year, they fly, they dance, they die. After this brief nuptial flight and the mating, the females return to the colony, or start a new one, first removing their own wings by eating them away. The poor old males, after this one brief mating, simply die, although many, many millions of them must anyway fall prey to the gulls, swifts and martins flying in a frenzy on this hot Summer day.

It is extraordinary that all the ants from thousands of different nests in an area are stimulated just for this very brief period, and their timing is undeniably immaculate. It seems to happen at the hottest time of the day, in the sort of conditions welcomed by glider pilots, when there are plenty of thermals of warm air. Could it be that the ants too need more than fragile wing power to gain height for their nuptial flight, that they too make use of the thermals to fly several thousand feet into the air?

The fact that the timing was so very precise on this occasion was only brought home to me the next morning. Those genial, assured men at the meteorological office had on the evening of the day of the ants, looked wisely at their weather charts, and, with all the aids of modern technology, had pronounced authoritatively that the fine weather would continue.

They couldn't have been more wrong. The morning was wet and windy, heavy rain continued for most of the day, and not even a crawling ant was to be seen anywhere. It certainly wasn't a flying day. Is it possible that the ants had somehow sensed that this one fine summer day was the 'do or die' day for their fateful flight?

Sea-gulls or Landlubbers?

'There must be rough weather brewing up in the Channel, all the sea-gulls have come inland.' So goes a piece of weather lore that is commonly quoted with all the assurance of an historic fact. It is a sweeping statement based on false reasoning. We've all watched the gulls following the plough or wheeling frantically above other farm machinery working the fields. I've seen them in great hoards, obscuring the tractor like a smutty snow storm, as a farmer drilled winter wheat. That sort of work produces only the slightest disturbance of the top soil, yet there they were grabbing not the valuable corn, but any worms or grubs turned over by the implement.

Even more impressive is the attraction for them of potato digging. As the prehistoric monster of a machine moves along the rows, like some ferris wheel given its freedom, spewing up the spuds, the gulls dive to the ground like well aimed arrows, each trying to be first on target, first to sample the newly turned soil.

Even a day later when all the crop has been bagged and carried away, some of the gulls return, maybe for a few small potatoes left behind, but more likely for the natural pickings.

Even though the old weather prophet may be right in his assumption of rough weather at sea, the gulls would have been on that potato field, fair conditions or foul. There's usually one snapshot in the family album, treasured for its sunny memories, of the great black-backed gull or the aggressive herring gull perched on a promenade railing—even the most amateur photographer with the cheapest of cameras can get that shot. But take a visit sometime to the self same spot in the depths of winter, and you will see that the gulls are far fewer in number. They were there in summer for the easy pickings, from the holiday rubbish that spills over from waste baskets on the sea front, or the litter we leave on the beaches. We, the sun seekers, have gone, so have the gulls because there's better rubbish elsewhere.

Rubbish is a great magnet for gulls. A large flock of them wheeling and diving on the outskirts of a large town means they've homed on to the local rubbish dump, making the journey to and from the same spot morning and night, following the same flight lanes on each trip as if guided by a pathfinder. They will feed the whole day through on the council rubbish tip or sewage farm, and, come evening, they'll wing back to their large communal roosts.

A visit to one of these roosts, on an off-shore island, reveals evidence, if ever it were needed, that gulls are indeed great scavengers. Plastic containers and other rubbish abound. All this debris could only have got there by air, and confirmation is provided by the occasional gull staggering in, with a can dangling, obviously picked up on a rubbish tip and now firmly wedged on the bird's foot.

Not all the gulls though seek out island refuges. Just as attractive to them are the inland sites; those great expanses of reservoir so necessary to maintain our water supplies. A large reservoir can be covered with thousands of gulls, as can open tracts of land like playing fields and aerodromes which, for the gulls, mean food and roosting sites.

It's not without reason then, that both military and civil airport authorities go to great lengths to prevent what are called 'bird strikes', the collision between flying aircraft and flying birds. Because radar can show up a flock of gulls on the screen, mid-air collisions are less of a hazard than they used to be. Much more dangerous is the aircraft landing or taking off which draws a gull weighing several pounds into a jet engine. Such a situation could cause a crash and loss of life, and will certainly kill the bird and do expensive damage to the engine.

This problem is tackled by persuading the gulls to leave the vicinity of the airfield. Some naval air stations rely on the natural antipathy of predator and prey by keeping falcons, and service personnel find themselves as falconers in uniform. Flying the falcons soon persuades gulls to move on elsewhere, even if only for a short time, but time enough for aircraft to take off or land. The other method is to use the natural distress calls of the birds. These are recorded on tape, and played back at the birds whenever they alight on runways. Unfortunately, familiarity with this treatment has bred contempt of it, and it has to be interspersed with other ruses.

Gulls, then, are the great opportunists of the bird world, and are often to be found nesting far inland, away from the rocks and the sea. Radnor forest, in Wales, provided a breeding site for a vast colony, although it's more than a stone's throw from salt water. Local people had the curious experience of collecting gulls' eggs, which are, we are led to believe, good eating, especially for those with rheumatic ailments—another tale to be taken with the pinch of salt that the sea-gulls seem to be able to do without.

Ferret It Out

The place of the rabbit in the country has changed over the years, particularly since the fifties when that ghastly disease, myxomatosis, decimated their population. Up until that time, millions of them cropped a living off grass, corn, and almost any small vegetation from around the edges of fields. Farmers knew only too well that their losses in those vital yards close to the hedgerows could only be balanced by keeping down the rabbits.

In a way though, what they lost on the corn swings they gained on the rabbit roundabouts, for it was quite common in some marginal hill farms to make a crop of the pests as well as the corn. Indeed there was a time when the sale of rabbits could just about meet the annual rent bill. Most were trapped, but some country folk reckoned that if the rabbits were going to take some of the profit from the soil, then they should, in return, provide sport.

For that reason most small holdings usually kept a couple of ferrets, one of each sex—a hob and a jill. A ferret is rather like an albino polecat, usually creamy white with pink eyes. It has two other distinctive features: an unsavoury smell, and a distinct liking for rabbits.

It used to be a very common sight to see two chaps dressed for a rough day. One would be carrying a spade, the other a makeshift box over his shoulder containing, of course, the ferrets. Ferreting is, on the face of it, a fairly simple matter. Having found a likely looking warren, all you do is to pop one ferret down the hole. The ferrets being what they are, soon search out the rabbits, which may then be caught in two ways.

The first, and least expensive, is to cover every single exit hole from the warren with nets. Usually when ferret and rabbit come face to face deep underground, the rabbit will bolt for the nearest exit, and into a tangle of net. There are certain problems with this method, because, no matter how carefully you have looked over the warren, there will almost always be one hole that hasn't been netted, and its from that tiny bolt hole the rabbit will scamper to freedom. Some people scorn such unsporting ways, and merely let the ferrets loose in the holes, retreating a few yards back with shotguns at the ready. In this case the rabbits have an even greater chance of getting away with it!

Ferreting is a tremendously efficient way of controlling rabbits, provided of course, the ferrets co-operate to the full. This is not always the case, since the ferret's one aim in life is to kill a rabbit. Once given its freedom in a warren, the ferret is not particularly concerned about the chaps hanging around outside waiting for the sport. The ferret goes in for the kill, and if the first rabbit it finds doesn't move quickly enough, then it's a goner. It is grabbed behind the neck and quickly and efficiently killed. That done, the ferret settles down for a meal and, after that, a sleep, much to the consternation of the sportsmen.

In this situation, they bring into play the second ferret, one that is known as a 'liner'. A small leather collar, with a long strong string attached, is placed round its neck, and with a bit of luck it will make straight for its mate, sleeping it off. This is where ferreting becomes hard work. There's nothing more frustrating than lying flat on your face, head stuffed in a rabbit hole, desperately listening for the slightest scuffle underground that will indicate the meeting of the ferrets. Once you've plotted the approximate whereabouts of ferrets and rabbit, then comes the slog of digging down to them. With large tree roots and small boulders in the way, it's often long and tedious and sometimes downright impossible.

All is not necessarily lost even by this stage—at least your ferrets aren't lost. The one attached to the line can be dragged gently back to daylight, and it will eventually reappear, blinking its pink eyes at the sun, its muzzle coated with blood. This is confirmation that ferret number one has killed. You can now either sit around, and wait for the ferret to come out in its own good time, or, a quicker ploy, put a dead rabbit into one entrance hole and block every other one up with a few sods of turf. This always supposes that the disaster hasn't happened at the first warren of the day, in which case you haven't a spare bunny to use as bait. In general, though, returning a few hours later and opening up the holes again will reveal a contented, but bloody ferret.

Unfortunately a bolt hole for a rabbit is a bolt hole for a ferret as well, and it could be that your precious rabbit-killer will find its freedom through that. One of the best ferrets we had was first spotted in the headlights of our car one evening along a narrow lane. No one ever claimed it, and it put in years of excellent service, not only in bolting a plentiful supply of rabbits, but also in siring not a few litters of responsive young.

Today rabbits are less subterranean than they once were, because those that survived the dreaded 'myxo' were the ones which lived above ground, in bramble thickets and tangles of bracken. The later generations, the ones which are multiplying again in many parts of the country, are not the burrowers their ancestors were. With this change in the habits of rabbits, there are fewer and fewer ferrets. Happily, though, in some parts, it's still possible to see a couple of country chaps intent on a day's ferreting, oblivious of the frustrations the next few hours may have in store for them.

'Who Wants an Oont-hill?'

Oont, hoont, wont, wunt, unt, want. You are not looking at a
pigmy tribal chant. These are the names of mole, an animal loved
by some and hated by others. Mole is, I think, a very useful animal,
but then I'm looking at him from the selfish standpoint of the gardener who finds in those hills of soil a ready made basic potting
mixture. This mixture needs only the addition of a few handfuls of
sand and peat to turn even the worst gardener in the world into a
Fred Streeter, with a fistful of green fingers.

Sad to say though, the mole has fallen foul of many gardeners
and workers of the soil over the years, just because of those tips that
he throws up to the surface as he works his way through his underground habitat. One would think that down there, under the turf,
mole wouldn't worry anyone. Now ask any farmer who has
blunted the cutting blades of his expensive machinery on stones
thrown up in a mole hill; ask him about the disturbance to newly
sown crops; ask the greenkeeper on a golf course or playing field;

ask the gardener, who has acres of green lawns to keep as trim as a bowling green. They'll all condemn the mole out of hand.

If ever there was a combination of elegance and tenacity, it must surely be the mole. If you get the chance to hold a live one, you'll see what I mean. His coat is pure velvet, wrapped around a little powerhouse vibrating with energy. He has, too, a certain charm, perhaps because you can't really see the eyes in all that fur. His coat covers him in a glossy sheen, that looks black in some lights, grey in others. Compared with this spankingly smart coat, the tail is rather apologetic—a tiny, light coloured stub that doesn't look as though it belongs.

Holding a mole in the hand is not that easy. It wriggles all the time, and, if it can't get free by nipping with very sharp teeth, it does have large front claws which are, in effect, very sharp, five-pointed shovels. These shovels are the reason for the success of the mole. The animal is shaped like a pointed, boring device, propelled by two outboard mechanical paddles. Like the miner working the coal face, the mole has to send what he has excavated to the surface, and thus makes hills. Large hills indicate the living quarters, or fortresses as they are called; smaller hills dot the route from the fortress to the feeding grounds, and by taking a line between two hills, it's an easy matter to locate the run. If, as you walk between the hills, the ground 'gives' under one foot, it means you've found the underground supply line. For all the mole does, is to collect worms at their own level, rather than digging for them from above.

Times were when the skin of this animal, which is only about six inches long, was much sought after in the fur trade; not, of course, for complete garments, but for trimming and decoration. To satisfy the needs of the trade, the trapper went about his business, satisfying in this way both farmer and furrier. Fortunately for both mole and trappers alike, mole is a crafty little creature, so there were always plenty of his number around the following year to keep everyone in work.

The trade eventually declined, the traditional trapper vanished and the moles thrived, although I'm not convinced that their numbers necessarily increased. I think it's another case where culling produces better conditions for the survivors, for, without so much competition for the available food supplies, a fitter and healthier stock results. That in turn, means a higher survival rate. Without control, any over-population is self-controlling in the long run.

Even though the mole-trapper had gone, control was still considered necessary by many people, and this I think, is one of the saddest, grimmest stories of post-war years. We turned to poisons to keep down the mole population. Not any old poison, but the most deadly, strychnine, was used. Small bottles of the stuff were kept in sheds and stores when they should have been placed in a really safe place, under lock and key. But then that's the way of many countrymen who tend to hide things away, like a squirrel. All sorts of unlikely places became the stores for strychnine, beams and rafters, the tiles in a barn. Some of those poisons are still probably there today, forgotten, but still potentially lethal.

Such hiding places are never really safe from inquisitive children at play, and how many tiny bottles, I wonder, have been dislodged by mice or rats? Even if the loss was discovered, how many people would admit to the carelessness of leaving strychnine lying around in an outhouse? The poison is laid down, incidentally, by dipping earthworms in it, and placing them in the mole run; with the animal's appetite for worms, the result is inevitable.

For the gardener with a small lawn that has been invaded by moles the best method is still, I think, the old fashioned, but highly efficient, trap. It's been in use for years and, compared with the 'gin', which caught rabbits and foxes by one leg and kept them in agony for hours, the mole trap was quick and humane.

It looks like a lobster claw, spring loaded and held apart by a small metal ring on a chain. It is a fiendishly simple device. When the trap is set in the run, the mole, pushing along, displaces the ring with its snout, the claw springs shut and breaks the mole's back in an instant. It is not completely efficient however. Many's the trapper who's come along on his early morning rounds to find that his traps are sprung, but empty. Careful examination of the run will show that the mole has come along to the trap and has dug a diversion round it; the excavation work springs the trap and the mole goes on his way, unharmed.

After several attempts to catch this crafty mole with no success, the trapper then resorts to trickery of his own, setting a second trap in the run a few inches away from the first one. The theory is that the mole, having found the first obstruction and dug a way round it, won't be expecting this second trap and will be caught. It sometimes works, but it is not infallible. I tried it once. Night after night the two traps were set in the run, morning after morning, it was the same story of sprung traps and no mole. Then, one morning I did have a catch—a weasel. This was an object lesson in a way, for had I left things alone, the weasel would have caught the mole for me.

There are said to be other ways of getting rid of moles, and one popular method is the planting of one of the euphorbias, caper-spurge, which is also known as the mole-tree. Many people I know have caper-spurge in their gardens and they have moles as well. I can't help thinking that somewhere along the line, we have mixed up our moles. The spurges have a milky sap when the stem is broken, and I can vouch for the fact that the juice from sun-spurge is a treatment for warts. I have also heard it said that the juice from caper-spurge is a remedy for that other blemish of the skin, moles. So the cure for a mole is not necessarily the remedy for an oont.

'Get down behind Low Cover'

Infantry instructors have a pretty turn of phrase. I can still hear the words ringing in my ears, pithy and to the point. 'Crawling around with your arse in the air, you'll look like a bleedin' camel to the enemy. Get a bullet there soldier, and you'll 'ave more than the 'ump.' They're words not easily forgotten, especially when real bullets are flying around. What our friendly instructor was trying to do, was instil in us the value of cover, getting around in open country without being seen, using folds in the terrain to keep out of sight, making the best available use of hedgerows. In some parts of the country though, the tactical use of hedgerows is well nigh impossible today.

Hedgerows have been disappearing at the rate of thousands of miles every year. The reasons are perfectly obvious to the farmers who must get the best possible return from their land. A small field unit of untidy shape is difficult to cultivate and costly to harvest; so the tendency is towards great prairies that can be ploughed by multi-furrow implements, and can be harvested by combines in convoy.

Removing hedges gives a greater acreage of land available for crops, and takes away a seed bed for the weed. Even in stock rearing country, the hedge is not as important as it was. There is no need now to shelter cattle at night from the chill winds and snows of winter. Those cattle are kept in cosy, warm buildings.

Hedges, too, are costly to maintain. Gone are the days when the farm labourer would spend the quiet time of the year, a sack over his shoulders to keep off the rain, going about the tedious business of hedging and ditching. There is no refuting the facts; hedges are economic burdens, unproductive luxuries.

However, removing hedges at the rate we've been going in the past thirty years has applied pressure in another direction, on our wildlife. An enormous number of species rely on hedges; small birds for nesting sites, and small mammals for shelter and food. One small section of hedge is often an important route on a wild-life communications system. It's exactly the same story as the infantryman using the hedge to keep behind cover, in wildlife terms, the same cover is used to get from one point to another without being seen by an enemy.

There's always an enemy somewhere; on the ground in the shape of fox or stoat sniffing the breeze, in the air a kestrel or buzzard scanning the ground for the slightest movement. In the constant battle between predator and prey, the hedge is one levelling factor. It is fortunate that many farmers and landowners have realised that perhaps the profit and loss balance sheet doesn't give the whole picture, and that there should be a bit of give and take as well as debit and credit. They've realised that, in these great prairies of theirs, there are still unproductive corners where machines can only manoeuvre with difficulty, or where the ground is too wet.

In some areas, they've been persuaded to do some giving, and have restored the balance to a certain extent by planting these useless corners with trees again, making in effect a series of mini-woodlands. Where this is done, we're seeing the birds and small mammals back again in some numbers. When they're on the move, they still have to make a dash from one tiny copse to the next, instead of wandering leisurely beneath the cover of the hedge that used to be there, or flying along its length. But at least these corners go a long way towards putting right some of the wrongs.

This picture of hedgerow destruction, it must be admitted, does not hold true for the whole country. On my travels through the beautiful border counties of Herefordshire and Radnorshire, for example, my heart always warms at the sight of their well kept thorn hedges. These are carefully laid out and trimmed, year in, year out, a running testament to fine craftmanship.

Pride is, of course, not the only reason for such maintenance. There are a lot of sheep in those counties, and woe betide any farmer in sheep country whose hedges become a bit thin, especially if the grazing in the fields is a little less lush than the grass on the roadside verges. If there isn't a hole in the hedge, an old Welsh ewe will soon make one to get at the greener grass on the other side. So where there are sheep, there are still good hedges, but I can't help wondering how long that will last. It would only take a swing towards intensive factory farming of lambs to shear the country-side of several thousand more miles of hedges.

In some parts of the country though, hedges are no longer 'made', they are mutilated. Instead of the man with a billhook, swiping his sweaty way along the hedgerow, there comes a man with an infernal machine. There he sits in his tractor seat, manipulating a great slicing machine that goes through the vegetation like a knife through butter, through anything from slender twigs to small tree trunks three or four inches thick. It is highly efficient and justifiable in economic terms. The hedge is trimmed to an even height and a symmetrical thickness, and will probably not want attention for another two or three years. But that machine leaves behind a veritable rubbish heap of timber. Wood galore is flailed all over the road, sharp, jagged pieces of wood that are a hazard to the traveller, be he motorist, cyclist or pedestrian.

While I accept that some hedges must, of necessity, be removed and that the management of those that remain is more economically viable when tackled with machinery, I do feel that the operations could be better timed in some parts. Along the lane from our village, the council workmen had been busy trimming up the face of the hedgerows, and, as I strolled along, I noticed in a bush the neatly rounded, hair-lined nest of a chaffinch. The blades of the machine had missed it by a couple of inches, and there it was, exposed and deserted. On a trip to Cambridgeshire in the spring of the same year, I noticed a hedge clearing operation going on, razing it to the ground right in the middle of the nest-building season.

It's worth remembering that some of our hedges first grew through birds perching on posts, and discarding seeds from plants and shrubs. Those seeds took root, and a hedge grew, perhaps we should repay their pains by taking some ourselves.

Birdies and Eagles

They stride resolutely across the rolling downland or weave their way through the sand dunes, a bag of clubs on their back or on a trolley. The golfers of the world are very privileged people who have paid out a lot of hard earned cash so that they may follow the royal and ancient game. Joining a club may cost a hundred pounds or more; buying the clubs costs as much again. Then there are those small white balls they hit with anger, frustration, or delight.

Those expensive little balls get lost by the score every day on most courses, and once found again by the greenkeeping staff or club professional, are very saleable items, much cheaper than buying a new ball still in its wrappings. When the game took up more of my time than it should have done, it was usually possible to buy secondhand balls from the greenkeeper at the Taunton and Pickeridge course for a matter of a few pence—much below the going rate. The only snag was that these balls were invariably even more pock-marked than is usual, and looked as if a small dog might have been playing with them.

Teeth marks they most certainly were, made by fox cubs. Parts of this course are bordered with thick clumps of blackthorn, and no man, not even a golfer down to his last ball could even venture into those thickets. Indeed the local pack of foxhounds have been known to give them a wide berth. Yet in the spring, a walk around the course in the early morning would reveal golf balls littered around like an overnight crop of mushrooms. They had been brought out from the blackthorn bushes by the fox cubs, played with and then left on the course where they more rightly belonged.

Golfers in their tens of thousands follow their game, keeping their eye on the ball, and seeing precious little else. Some of them return to the clubhouse complaining bitterly that they have been put off their game yet again by the deafening flutter of butterfly wings. They talk of their birdies and eagles, but for most of them they see their course as nothing more than an area of the countryside which they are entitled to use as the whim takes them.

On the face of it, the odds are all against any other life taking advantage of the vast acres of a course. It's managed from the first tee to the eighteenth green with meticulous care, fertilizers go on it by the hundredweight, weedkiller by the gallon, and worm-killers by the quart. Yet, despite all these attempts to make a stretch of countryside useful only to a select band of sportsmen, it works the other way. Often without realising it, the golfers are using, many would say selfishly, some of the finest nature reserves in the country.

Perhaps that's why my game of golf never reached the dizzy heights of single handicap figures. My attention, which should have been on that miserable little ball, was on other things. Who could possibly concentrate on hitting the ball on a hazy, maysy afternoon while nightingales trilled and sang in the woods alongside the fairways; while larks rose higher and higher into the blue of the sky in that fantastic song that never, it seems, allows time for breath? I've even pretended to look for a ball, when, in truth, I've been searching for the lark's nest after seeing the bird leave.

Practically every single yard of a golf course or links makes an ideal habitat for something or other. The fairways are gangmown every week of the summer. It's only the lush green grass, close cropped, that the greenkeeper wants to see, yet despite his efforts common orchids come up in profusion—a bit on the stunted side, which is not surprising in the circumstances—but reappearing year after year. That same fairway, too, is good for a breakfast of mushrooms if you could get out there early enough!

For some strange reason I've never met a golfer who reacted violently against mushrooms on the course, even though he has often walked purposefully and mistakenly forward to a white speck in the distance thinking it to be his ball. Some flowers too, produce the same optical illusion on a links course. There it's possible to find clumps of burnet roses, delicate and pale cream, hugging the ground where no machine can harm them. They may be slightly tattered in some cases, where a golfer has taken a violent swing at his ball lodged in their midst, but they are resilient enough to withstand even that treatment.

Every course I know has something different to offer: fox cubs, badger sets, nesting birds galore. There is in fact, one bird that golfers do notice. On many courses the crows are enemy number one, not because they take the eggs of young, smaller birds, but because they are wont to fly down and pick up golf balls before the golfer can get to them. Some golfers I know have been heard to say they intend carrying a .410 shot gun in their bag of equipment.

Butterflies, those noisy wing-beating insects, thrive on many courses, and here again, you would have thought that the use of some sprays would have killed them off. Not a bit of it. One course I know would boast, if it knew, of a regular explosion of marbled white butterflies every year.

Even as the days of summer give way to autumn, and the fruits of the hedgerows take on their ripe hues, so these precious acres become stopping-off points and feeding places for many of the migrant birds. Hawthorns, which make popular boundary hedges, with their crop of haws attract the fieldfares and redwings on their way south. The crop is cleared in a matter of days as the birds top up before moving on.

A golf course may be a preserve of golfers, but it is also a reserve without par. In these days of high land prices and greater concern for the better use of our land resources, the day may come when the golfers of the world may have to share their courses with people of other interests, perhaps because they can no longer afford to have the exclusive use of a particular piece of the countryside.

I can feel the hackles rising. I know only too well the antagonism that exists where it so happens that a course is also common land, where sheep, cattle, even goats, graze on and around the fairways, where people picnic and exercise their dogs. The two interests don't mix, but the day may not be very far away when they will have to. That surely is better than seeing a golf course disappear under the concrete jungle of a housing estate. If that happens, we should have lost not just an exclusive club, but another nature reserve as well.

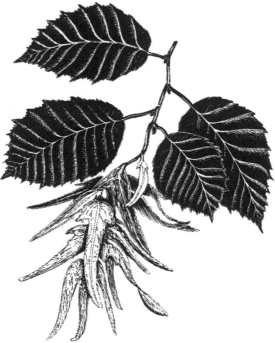

'Peace on Earth'

Just at the time of the year when most people are full of kind thoughts and goodwill towards their fellow men, I tend to get a bit sad. It's not the thought of all those ghastly bills that will have to be paid on the first day of the New Year. It's rather the fact that, while everyone pays lip service to peace on earth, half the population of the country seem intent on taking a piece of the earth. They want to steal, and that's the only word for it, some of the growing parts of the countryside to satisfy their desire for free decoration at home.

There is a place that I pass by regularly on my walks, a deserted spot where, probably, no one else goes except the farmer to leave a bale or two of hay for his store cattle. Anyway, at this spot, there is a large holly tree. It doesn't have many berries on it, even in a good year, and occasionally the farmer chops down a branch, quite scientifically, so that he doesn't unbalance the tree. I imagine he sells that branch in the local market, and after all, why shouldn't he? He can claim, quite rightly, that the tree is on his land, and, if it produces a crop for which there is a ready sale, then he is entitled to profit by it.

Other holly trees I know are more accessible, to their detriment. They used to be holly trees, but are now dead, grey statues, standing in memory of our greed. Inevitably their plinth is the roadside hedge. In their younger days, they have borne berries in profusion, great masses of fine red fruit, and shiny green leaves, but every year, on almost the same day, such trees become denuded and defoliated as more and more branches are hauled down by the passing motorist. The tree slowly dies, and, one day, the man who has made a habit of obtaining his Christmas decorations from that spot, will come along again and blame pollution for the death of his tree.

There are thousands of trees just like that one, all over the country. They have been ravaged because we look upon a sprig of green holly with bright red berries, as a symbol of Christmas. After a few days, of course, in the warmth of our homes, the berries shrivel and make a mess around the home; the green leaves become brittle and brown, and, once the twelve festive days are over, the holly is taken down from picture rails and mantlepieces and consigned to the flames of the lounge fire.

It is this point that many people find to their cost just how inflammable dried holly is, as the flames leap high up the grate and a neighbour comes rushing in to bring the glad tidings that the chimney is on fire. Those sprigs of holly flare like greasy paper. What is brought into our homes as the symbol of the crown of thorns can be highly dangerous for this reason, but there's one other very good argument for leaving holly branches where they grow. Their berries are part of the last resort larder of many of our birds, a source of food in the hard times of the winter, when the rest of the cupboard is bare.

The same is true of other so-called Christmas decorations, like mistletoe. That plant may be regarded as a symbol of peace, but it is also a food source for birds. Fortunately, much of the mistletoe

that grows in the countryside is so difficult to reach that it gets left alone, particularly as it is often found in the tops of tall trees like poplars. Once again, it is the poor farmer who suffers. It's another case of a quick leap over his orchard fence and a bunch of mistletoe being thrown into the car boot. Often the apple trees are damaged by the thief, and another small item of legitimate income disappears. Christmas trees are another illegally harvested Christmas decoration. Hundreds are stolen from plantations every year.

Of course, there are things we can collect from the countryside without causing damage or annoyance. I can't think of anyone objecting to the removal of a few strands of ivy from a roadside hedge or tree. I know that if we take the idea of conservation to extremes, even the ivy should be left alone; for insect life finds shelter in the nooks and crannies between the ivy stem and the tree-trunk, and the berries of ivy too, are useful food for some birds. Another attractive and harmless way of decorating the house is to use the heads of dead flowers. Plants like teazles, for instance, make excellent decoration, and, by the time Christmas comes around, the dead flower heads will have been cleared of seeds by the finches.

No one wants to cast a wet blanket over our homes at Christmas, but let's all try a little moderation. There is no need to strip the country bare of holly and mistletoe, and it's worth remembering that whatever we think will make a useful and colourful decoration, probably belongs to someone. Seeing a holly tree on a farmer's land may provoke us to go and take some of the branches, but it is far better to approach the farmer, and ask the price of a few sprigs. He might refuse to consider the idea, but the chances are that, with peace in mind, he'll probably be prepared to give some away.

Which Way Now?

An evening drive across rural England in early autumn is a depressing experience, as billowing clouds of smoke stretch for miles over the arable prairies. Tongues of flame creep ever on in relentless destruction, consuming a commodity we apparently cannot use, that disposable aftermath of the harvest, straw. Within a few days of harvest-home, happy congregations gather in village churches and chapels, stacked high with the fruits of their toil and give their thanks for the bounty and the blessing. 'All is safely gathered in' rings through the rafters, while the last acrid smells of a scorched earth policy hang in the air to remind us that we've only been partly successful in our gathering.

The time is fast approaching in a world of spiralling populations, when we shall not be able to waste anything. It will be a matter of survival, not economy. There must be a use somewhere for straw, even if it means taking a backward step to the days when straw and hay, cut as chaff and mixed with mangolds, kept hungry farm stock in reasonable fettle during the winter months. It may not have been as nutritious as today's protein laden 'cake', but it was good enough. Soon, the foodstuffs now used to produce animal food—the fish-meal, the soya-flour, the maize and the corn—will be needed to feed us directly, and not second-hand as meat which has been fattened on that protein.

More and more farmers are realising that cramming the maximum stock population into their meagre acres is no longer sensible or even economical. They look at the price of the artificial fertilisers necessary to keep grass growing lush for as many months as possible; they look at the cost of 'concentrates'; they look at the way they've specialised in recent years on one aspect of farming.

In those red and black figures, they see the warning signs as clearly as they see their straw burning, as clearly as they see their herds diminishing. Perhaps there will be another revolution in farming, perhaps there will be a return to the traditional mixed farm, where one crop supported another, where indeed the whole complex was inter-related. Perhaps the ranks of the 'muck and magic' brigade will become an army rather than a small platoon, and those who fervently believe in the ideals and benefits of organic farming, of putting back into the soil the natural nutrients produced on the farm itself, those people will come into their own.

Just as we are getting around to the idea of recycling our waste, so we must, in the long term, look hard at the natural waste that's going on all round us. There are thousands of acres of herbage that go unharvested every year. These are not compact, collective acres; they are small patches of land that grow grass that could be helpful; these are the sections of road that have been straightened out in the interests of safety, and are reverting to natural vegetation. There they stand, cut back by local authorities for perhaps six feet, and the remainder left.

All this is very commendable from a plant conservation point of view, but there's no reason why the whole section shouldn't be cut as hay. In some parts of the country, such pickings are happily gleaned by the romanies to feed their horses, or by the marginal smallholder to eke out his own supplies. Today, however, there are more and more of those waste areas on the banks alongside our motorways. It wouldn't need much ingenuity to reap an even bigger harvest there. The end result might not be as good as a meadow fertilised into production, but it could make a significant contribution.

It is not only the farmers who are having second thoughts. More and more of us are going back to the joys of growing our own fruit and vegetables; allotments, neglected over the years, are coming back into production to help balance our own household accounts,

to offset rising costs. Perhaps, in the long term, our new houses may look the same, except that what we used to call the garage will be the 'store'—the place to keep the produce we've grown in ground where roses used to flourish. It won't be like the store shed of a country cottage, which is nothing more than a frost free lean-to; our store will be purpose-built to combine the traditional with the modern. Storage bins and slatted shelves will stand alongside the deep-freeze cabinets.

Once this attitude is generally accepted, we can look forward to some profound changes in our way of life, some pleasant, some not so pleasant, but all crucial to our mutual welfare. Chimneys and fireplaces may be a standard feature of new houses, so that wood, as well as coal, can supplement the 'clean' fuels. Pets, particularly dogs, may become increasingly rare because they drain food resources and are a health risk; one serious outbreak of rabies would certainly diminish the popularity of our 'best friend'. All in all we may find, that, if we take the right turning, we will be singing, 'All is safely gathered in,' with real conviction.

And Things That Go Bump

'What's the weather going to do today Bert?' There's always a local whose pet bunion, damp piece of sea-weed or general country knowledge will supply the absolutely certain answer. 'Well Sir, round here we do say that if it baint rainin' you should take your mac, and if it is, you can please yersel'.' A bit of bet-hedging country logic that is only surpassed by the other weather prophet who doesn't believe everything he hears, and informs you quite seriously, 'My wireless reckoned it's going to rain today. What did your's say?'

Hearing, believing, thinking, are three steps to the real country-man, as inseparable as the Freeman, Hardy and Willis who made his boots. If you want to put your knowledge of the countryside to the test, try taking a walk through a wood of a winter night, the sort of night with a high wind blowing, and clouds in phantom shapes moving across the face of a half moon.

For your own peace of mind, if not self-preservation, take a path that you have followed in daylight. You won't really recognise it as you stand at the edge of the wood, one moment in pitch darkness that envelopes you like a shroud, the next in grotesque shadow, but you're not faint hearted, and so you take a few steps along the path. You know the way, you've walked it before. You know where that old stump of an oak tree is, in fact, you've tripped over it on several occasions. . . but that was in daylight.

Take just three or four steps and stand still for a minute or so to get your bearings, and let your eyes become accustomed to the changing light of the night. . . stand still, look and listen.

The trees are as bare as skeletons—not a leaf on the oak, the ash or the beech, only on that tree over there. It must be a holly, it has an overcoat, one moment jet black in the moonlight, the next invisible in the dark.

Eyes begin to focus now, so. . .another step into the wood.

There's a crack like a pistol shot. You duck. You can't help it. A poacher up to no good, bagging a cock pheasant from it's roost? That shot, if shot it was, was so close that he can't be more than a couple of feet from you. You try to come to terms with yourself, hardly daring to breath, hearing only your heart beating out a tattoo. Your feet won't move. They're rooted to the ground as surely as the giant oak by your side, until at last one foot comes free, and you take another step, and another, touching the ground as gingerly as if you were walking on thin ice. The pistol cracks again, and this time you feel it, right underneath your feet. A twig, dry as tinder, that snapped as you stepped on it.

That problem solved, your confidence returns, and you're just about to walk on, when fear grips you like a vice. There's a tap-tap-tapping sound behind you. The leaves on the ground rustle like . . . like a man following you, with a stick in his hand . . .

The mind begins to play tricks. Is there someone else around after all? It must have been a poacher, it wasn't a twig snapping. This is no place for you. The poacher can have the wood to himself. But the tapping sound goes on without getting any closer, keeping metronomic time with your own heart.

Hearing, believing, thinking. Work it out, think clearly, apply that logical mind to the problem. Up there, right above your head, that's where the sound is coming from, and the sigh of relief you breathe is louder than the wind. Two trees stand close together. A slender branch from one beats a gentle tattoo against the trunk of the other. That's explained the walking stick, but what about the rustle of the leaves? Nothing more than a rabbit probably, even a tiny vole. Sounds are magnified beyond belief on nights like these.

Just at that moment, you hear a clap of thunder. But you think logically, and at this moment, you really feel you're winning. You realise there was no flash of lightning. The sound came from that big black tree, the one you've decided long ago is a holly. It's a pigeon, disturbed from it's roost, more scared than you are. The thunder? That was just the flap of its wings as it flew out of the tree.

After that piece of work you can almost feel the countryman's medal being pinned onto your chest. You've passed the test. Then you notice the silence, a silence you can feel as the wind dies down, and takes with it all the sound that had your mind playing tricks. You realise that even quiet can be all enveloping, as claustrophobic as darkness, gripping you, pressing you down, pushing you into an abyss.

Suddenly it's shattered by a scream that echoes off the walls of your self-made chasm. It goes through you like a knife, again and again. . .

Some years ago I lived deep in a Somerset wood, approached only by a steep, mile-long track. A cousin came to stay for the weekend, glad to find peace and quiet in the countryside, away from the workaday city world. But, during her first night in the house, that same sound, that eerie scream went on for fully half an hour. The next morning my cousin's bedroom window was tightly shut. She looked a bit pale, but then she wasn't used to country sounds, and certainly hadn't ever heard anything like that painful screaming on a cloud-scudding January night.

It's the most frightening sound that you will hear echoing from depths of a wood—a love-lorn vixen screaming her mating call. If that's what you've decided that you heard on your midnight stroll, full marks and home to your bed.

If, by chance, there are strange noises during the night, up there above your head in the roof—scratches and scuffles, and hoppity-hop footfalls—that get louder and louder as the night wears on, don't worry. It's probably only a couple of mice, or a rat, or maybe even a starling. Probably . . . Sleep well, and don't forget to shut the window, tightly.

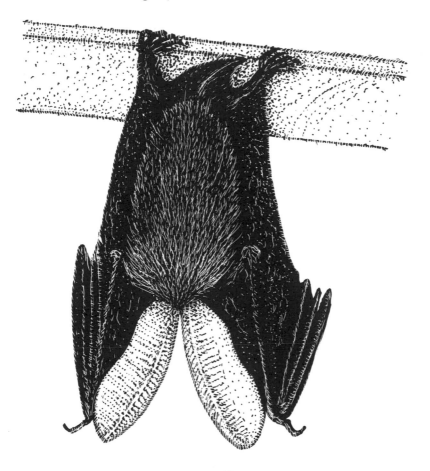